"Pastor Kim has a righ _ generation. We know the perso the preacher, and we've seen the preacher behind the pulpit—she is the real deal!"

—PASTORS WILEY AND JEANA TOMLINSON
NEW COVENANT MINISTRIES
JACKSONVILLE, FLORIDA

"Our very good friend, Kim Daniels, is a special trophy of God's grace. She has always done everything with excellence. She was a superb sinner, grasping after all the world had to offer. She was a magnificent athlete, training hard and striving to be the best and the fastest. But now she is an outstanding Christian servant of God, aggressively working with the hard cases in the tough places. She is one of Satan's worst enemies to be sure. You will fall in love with Kim as you read her book."

—DR. C. PETER AND DORIS WAGNER
PRESIDENT, GLOBAL HARVEST MINISTRIES
COLORADO SPRINGS, COLORADO

PN,
As I was readin' my copy of this book, the Lord showed me four people to bless with a copy. You were one of them, whatever the reason be for me givin' you one, I pray that it's revealed to you, as you read the book. Love, me

FROM A
MESS
TO A MIRACLE

BY KIMBERLY DANIELS

CREATION
HOUSE
PRESS

FROM A MESS TO A MIRACLE

FROM A MESS TO A MIRACLE
by Kimberly Daniels
Published by Creation House Press
A part of Strang Communications Company
600 Rinehart Road, Lake Mary, Florida 32746

Unless otherwise noted, Scripture quotations are from the King James Version of the Bible.

Scripture quotations marked AMP are from the Amplified Bible. Old Testament copyright © 1965, 1987 by the Zondervan Corporation. The Amplified New Testament copyright © 1954, 1958, 1987 by the Lockman Foundation. Used by permission.

Library of Congress Catalog Card Number: 2002108643
International Standard Book Number: 0-88419-935-5

Printed in the United States of America
03 04 05   6 5 4 3

Dedication

I dedicate this book to God's child of promise, my son Michael (Mike Mike). You were the only child I raised in the world, and I know it was not easy. I thank God for His grace and mercy over your life. Despite everything the enemy has sent your way, you stood to glorify the name of the Lord. You have a great spiritual heritage. Whatever you do, never let the enemy cut it off. It is yours! Always continue the flow of God in your bloodline, and be an example to your younger brothers and sisters. Remember, they are always watching you.

Thank you for putting up with me when I did not know the Lord, and even the times when you did not understand me when I did. Congratulations on your great accomplishment. We know it is all God, but He used you, Mike. You were in place to grab the baton of the generational blessings. Rejoice; the generational curse is broken, and as your mother, I speak the blessings of Abraham over every area of your life and bestow honor upon you as a mighty man of valor.

Your mom,
Pastor Kim

Table of Contents

Foreword

I've often testified of God's awesome ability to transform a sordid mess into a magnificent miracle. Kim Daniels, a woman who knows firsthand God's innumerable capabilities, boldly yanks the cover from the enemy's camp and exposes his deeds of darkness.

For too long the church has been fearful of confronting the blatant acts of demonic activity, but today God is raising up modern-day John the Baptists who are not afraid to cry loud and spare not. Her in-your-face ministry of confronting and annihilating the kingdom of darkness while maintaining godly humility has allowed her gift to be continually nurtured by God as a vessel to set the captives free.

She has an uncanny way of seeing the nature of

animals and comparing them to the supernatural attributes of demonic forces. Through this revelation knowledge she is able to psychoanalyze spiritually your demonic attack by identifying the root of it while simultaneously getting you set free. I've worked with Kim Daniels for a number of years and know that *From a Mess to a Miracle* is a very timely topic and a much-needed wake-up call for the entire body.

For years I've confronted the spirit of "lesbos," which is actually a spirit of control and manipulation. As perversion and immorality seem to become more of the acceptable norm, the body of Christ must be bold enough to take a stand. Romans 1:21 says, "Because that, when they knew God, they glorified him not as God, neither were thankful; but became vain in their imaginations, and their foolish heart was darkened."

Kim Daniels not only confronts vain imaginations that entice one to a quagmire of confusion, but she also leads the reader to the source of liberation. For many, the transition from the world to the church can often be very intimidating, confusing and misleading, but she enlightens the readers through words of comfort to hold on to their liberation and avoid being entangled again in the yoke of bondage. She explains that it is not tradition and religion that the individual needs to be introduced to, but rather the person of Jesus Christ. As she informs you of your ability through Christ to not only discern but also to dispel the deeds of darkness, you will become empowered to turn very messy situations into a message for God.

As you read the pages of this book, you will be set free from the spirit of fear, intimidation, perversion and other ungodly strongholds that desire to leave you dangling in a holding pattern and to prevent you from being planted on a solid foundation. You will realize that you no longer have to wrestle with demonic forces and accept the cards dealt to you when satan is the dealer. Remember, you control the game. Though the enemy creates the mess, you have the power to provoke the miracle!

From a Mess to a Miracle is a powerful reminder that you have been given "power to tread on serpents and scorpions, and over all the power of the enemy: and nothing shall by any means hurt you" (Luke 10:19) when you know who you are in Christ. Though the weapon may form, you have the power to determine how far it can prosper.

—BISHOP GEORGE G. BLOOMER
SENIOR PASTOR
BETHEL FAMILY WORSHIP CENTER
DURHAM, NORTH CAROLINA

Chapter I

THE MESSAGE

Orlando, Florida, is known all over the world as a vacation retreat. I had been to this city many times with my family, but this visit was no relaxing getaway. I was scheduled to speak at the annual Church of God Florida women's retreat, and I was terrified. Everything around me seemed enlarged, and I felt so small. The hotel where I was staying seemed like a huge mountain, and the conference was larger than any I had ever attended. My heart was racing.

I had arrived late and did not have time to check into my room. Pastor Joy, one of my mentors in the church, met me at the front door to let me know I had only fifteen minutes before the meeting started. Women were everywhere, wearing big, pretty hats in every color of the rainbow. My heart began to beat even faster as I mentally counted the number of women in attendance.

The halls were so crowded that a small traffic jam made it impossible to get into the room where my workshop was being held. As I moved hesitantly toward the door, I silently hoped someone would announce: "There has been a mistake. Kim Daniels is not really the speaker!" I turned to Pastor Joy and asked her to step into the restroom with me. As we entered, I told her I was so afraid I could hardly breathe. She prayed for me, and though my heart slowed down, my mind was still moving ninety miles an hour.

As we walked into the workshop room, I noticed that there were more than two hundred women present. I had been assigned to teach about moving from a mess to a miracle. Sister Miller, the state overseer's wife, was confident this was the message I was to minister, but I was still nervous. I knew only two people in the building: Sister Miller and Pastor Joy.

When I could no longer prolong things, I found myself standing behind the pulpit. As I opened my mouth, the women in the room drew to the Jesus in me. With no seminary training and no church upbringing, all I had to offer them was Jesus. I did not know the rules, and I could not see how I could ever fit in. Knowing I had received a sure word from the Lord helped me deal with my differences.

I opened by telling the women that I was certain I looked different to them, but they also looked a little strange to me. As the crowd laughed, the ice was broken, and we got to know each other by the spirit. God dealt with me about the title, "From a Mess to a

Miracle," and showed me that this was not just a message, as my natural mind would conceive it. Sister Miller gave the assignment, but the orders to preach this word came directly from heaven.

Without transformation there can be no dedication.

God opened up Romans 12 in a new realm. He began to speak to me about transformation. You see, this is what salvation is about. Without transformation there can be no dedication, and God will not accept anything less than total dedication to Him. According to the Book of Romans, the number one enemy of transformation is conformation. Romans 12:2 clearly tells us that we are not to be conformed to the things of the world, but transformed.

The devil is an infiltrator and works as an inside operator. He knows that as people of God we will not openly go to satan's den to worship, so he places the tools of his kingdom in the midst of the church. When we compromise to the spirit of the world in the house of God, we conform to the world. We become victims of the matrix, which is the world system, and we become subject to the god of this world.

> In whom the god of this world hath blinded the minds of them which believe not, lest the light of the glorious gospel of Christ, who is the image of God, should shine unto them.
>
> —2 CORINTHIANS 4:4

I was launched into a new level when God showed me that my autobiography, *Against All Odds*, was my testimony on the streets, but my testimony in the church was being transformed "from a mess to a miracle." People need to know that although God may have miraculously saved and delivered them, they must still allow Him to clean up the mess they made while they were in the world. We are born again, but there are situations from our past that are still unsaved. The fact is, there are some things that are impossible to save or salvage.

To salvage something is to save or rescue it. After a hurricane, the victim tries to salvage all that can continue to be used. We may as well face the fact that after we come out of the storm of living in the world, there is a lot that can never be salvaged and brought into the kingdom with us. Things try to follow us from the world in an attempt to make us struggle with a lukewarm lifestyle for Christ. A lukewarm temperature is a result of mixing hot and cold. We cannot mix the curses behind us with the blessings ahead of us. In the Bible, God instructed His people to put the blessing on one mountain and the curse on the other.

> And it shall come to pass, when the Lord thy God hath brought thee in unto the whither thou goest to possess it, that thou shalt put the blessing upon mount Gerizim, and the curse upon mount Ebal.
> —DEUTERONOMY 11:29

It is futile to attempt to live victorious in Christ with old ways following us like dark shadows. In Ephesians 4, we are told to: (1) put off the things that concern the old man; (2) be renewed in our minds; and (3) to put on the new man. These three principles are a road map to victorious living. When we lay down the old man it helps us to live saved. On the other hand when we put on the new man, it helps the people we come in contact with stay saved after they deal with us.

The reason many saints cannot adapt to a stable, Christlike lifestyle is because they are trying to save issues from their pasts that cannot be salvaged. These issues must be given to God so He can remove them from our lives. We have a great part in this deliverance, but only God is the true deliverer. As we humble ourselves and allow God to show us the areas in our lives that need to be dealt with, we will receive the power to resist the devil, and he will flee!

> But he giveth more grace. Wherefore he saith, God resisteth the proud, but giveth grace unto the humble. Submit yourselves therefore to God. Resist the devil, and he will flee from you.
>
> —JAMES 4:6–7

We must allow Jesus to clean out the mess of our past. If this does not happen, our past troubles will infiltrate our present deliverance. This is why people cannot declare the blessing of "being free indeed." Because of the precious blood of Jesus Christ, any mess the devil has placed in my life when I served him has already been approved to work out for my good now that I am saved. The key is that I have to be born again first!

There are a lot of things that leave us after we accept Christ; other things leave after we are delivered and filled with the Holy Spirit. I want to target the issues that need to be dealt with after that. We may as well be honest with ourselves: Even after deliverance and the infilling of the Holy Ghost we still have some things that God needs to deal with. Paul said that when he tried to do right, evil was always buffeting him.

> I find then a law, that, when I would do good, evil is present with me.
>
> —ROMANS 7:21

If we do not learn from our mistakes, we will go through them again.

I believe that this book is a testimonial and spiritual warfare tool for victorious living that will make a difference in your life if you allow it. I have to be transparent and tell about some of my church mess so you can really appreciate my miracle. As we walk with God, we will make many mistakes along the way, but a mistake is only a waste of time when we do not learn from it. If we do not learn from our mistakes, we will go through them again. I pray that you will learn from some of the things I have been through so you will not have to go through them, too. On the other hand, there are some things you will never understand until you experience them first-hand. At least this book can help you know you are not going crazy while you are going through them.

My autobiography was originally going to be titled *From a Mess to a Miracle,* but God said no because that would be the title of my next book. The fact of the matter is that there was a whole bunch of mess that I had to come out of before I could deliver this message. This was a new kind of mess. It was religious, obscure and smiled in your face. When the odds were against me on the streets, I could curse people and fight. On the streets we usually knew who our enemies were. It was hard, but it was real.

This new kind of mess was hypocritical back-stabbing and backbiting. I will never forget when Emma McDuffie prophesied to me before a crowd in my city. She said, "Yea, little dreamer, your brothers and sisters are about to throw you in the pit because of the vision." The next week another prophet said he saw me surrounded by snakes.

I thought the most loving people in the world surrounded me. They did not have names like "Dragon" and "Killer." These people did not deal drugs and carry illegal weapons with a mind to use them. These people did not stay out all night in the clubs and curse and brawl. They carried Bibles, and they hung out at Christian conferences. But I soon discovered that some people were more dangerous with Bibles than the jack-man was with a .45 caliber.

Dealing with this new kind of mess was like boxing with shadows. The apostle Paul said he did not fight as one beating the air; he had a definite enemy.

> I therefore so run, not as uncertainly; so fight I, not as one that beateth the air.
>
> —1 CORINTHIANS 9:26

In the crack house they have a term called "ghosting." This means that you know something is there, but you cannot see what it is. This is how I felt in

7

certain situations I faced in the body of Christ. I knew something was opposing me, but I all I saw in the natural were smiling faces. My spirit was telling me that something was wrong, but my mind said I was just being judgmental.

I remember when I first found out that everyone in the church was not born again. I thought to myself, *How can I deal with this kind of mess and stay saved?* Today, I stand in victory praising Jesus Christ! He sent a word that answered the question in my mind. He said, "Be not conformed!" Tradition and religion are not of God; therefore, they are of the world. Tradition is repetitive, and religion is an enemy of revival. These two strongmen come into the church under disguise.

God described the children of Israel as a stiff-necked people. The spirit that stabilizes its grip on the neck of its victim is Leviathan. A monstrous sea creature known for its ferocious strength, Leviathan represents a strongman that is "a king over all the children of pride" (Job 41:34). It is important that Christians understand how this spirit operates.

1. **His scales are his pride (Job 41:15).**
   These scales are knit so closely together that no air can come between them. The word *air* is *rûwach* in the Hebrew, and it represents the wind of revival. The scales of pride are enemies of revival. God could not move the people of Israel forward because of their stiff necks. A stiff neck will hinder the move of God.

2. **He beholds all high things (Job 41:34).**

The Hebrew word for *beholdeth*, *raw-aw*, means "to joyfully look upon and hold in place." Second Corinthians 10 refers to "every high thing that exalts itself against the knowledge of God." The word *high* is *hupsoma* in the Greek, and it means for someone to put himself in an elevated place or to have an elevated attitude. Leviathan is the latch for the high thing. He looks upon it with joy and secures it in place.

3. **His heart is as firm as a stone (Job 41:24).**
   A manifestation of pride and rebellion is hardness of heart. Rebellion is as the sin (or act) of witchcraft. (See 1 Samuel 15:23.) A rebel is a witch (the person doing the act). The epistles of Peter and James remind us that God resists the proud. This means He opposes and set Himself against the proud. God never comes up against Himself. If He opposes it, it is from the other side.

4. **His strength is in his neck (Job 41:22).**
   The Hebrew word for *neck* is *tsâvvâ'rah*, and it refers to the back of the neck where the yoke is lodged. Isaiah speaks of the day when the burden shall be removed from the shoulder and the yoke from off the neck. (See Isaiah 10:27.)

5. **He is a "piercing serpent" and a "crooked serpent" (Isaiah 27:1).**
   The term *piercing* means that this is a fugitive

spirit. The spirit of pride tends to make people unstable. They run from place to place like a vagabond or transient. The word *crooked* means "winding spirit" or "wrong way." One of the strongest manifestations of pride is the desire to be right. Pride can never take the blame and always needs an alibi. The crooked serpent always leads its victim in the wrong direction. The piercing serpent and the crooked serpent often walk in a threefold cord with religion.

The spirit of pride is the underlying enemy that gives feet to the backsliding spirit. Even when a person thinks about coming back to God, pride ensures and secures his or her steps.

It seems so simple, yet so difficult. God tells us not to be like the world, but the threefold cord of the world attempts to draw everything in us to it. We deceive ourselves when we think satan and his kingdom will not tempt us. The Bible says we must be careful that when we think we stand, we do not fall. In Matthew 4, Jesus was tempted in the wilderness. What was He tempted with? He was tempted with the threefold cord of the world: (1) power, the counterfeit to the anointing ("Command that these stones be made bread"); (2) fame, the counterfeit to true evangelism ("Son of God, cast thyself down"); and (3) mammon, the counterfeit to true prosperity ("All these things will I give thee").

For the purposes of this study, let us compare the spirit of Leviathan to the threefold cord of the world.

✧ **The lust of the flesh**—the *religious spirit* that attempts to serve God through the flesh realm

✧ **The lust of the eye**—the *crooked spirit* that sees things the way it pleases

✧ **The pride of life**—the *piercing* (fugitive) *spirit* that always flees from God

Leviathan has always been a major strongman in the world. In the last days this spirit is even more rampant. Despite this, Isaiah 27:1 says that there will be a day of reckoning. God will punish Leviathan and slay him in the sea. What do we do in the meantime? We should treat Leviathan like any other devil; resist him and he *will* flee!

Back at the women's retreat, I was finally up preaching. My appearance was a sharp contrast to the women in the crowd. I was wearing earrings and a pantsuit amid a sea of women who do not wear pants, and I had five gold teeth shining brightly in my mouth. But when the anointing came in the room, whether or not I would be received was no longer an issue. The anointing demanded that they receive Jesus.

The eyes of the women in that room lit up as I began preaching. It was as if I could hear them thinking, *We have never heard anything like this before.* That is the fruit of transformation. When God transforms us into what He wants us to be, it cannot be duplicated. True transformation causes a uniqueness to manifest in our ministries that only Jesus Himself can get the glory for.

In order for us to be transformed, God has to make some changes in our lives. This seems to be the most difficult part of answering the call of God—letting Him make the changes. He has to take some things away and move some things around. It is never comfortable when God is making changes because all of hell is trying to get us to stay where we are. The enemy wants us to see the church as one big copy machine, but God is killing the spirit of duplication.

The greatest attribute of the apostolic is that it does not conform.

This is why He saved the restoration of the apostolic ministry for the last days. The apostles have been suppressed as if they no longer exist in the capacity that they operated in during the New Testament. I declare that these are the days when apostles are emerging to set order, declare and release. The greatest attribute of the apostolic is that it does not conform. It is not moved by the status quo or how things have always been done.

As a matter of fact, the apostolic anointing of God does just the opposite. It demands that everything that is out of the order of God line up. It is a shaking anointing! The scripture that declares that everything that can be shaken will be shaken so everything that cannot be shaken will remain has a whole lot to do with the restoration of the apostolic.

12

And this word, Yet once more, signifieth the removing of those things that are shaken, as of things that are made, that those things which cannot be shaken may remain.

—Hebrews 12:27

God shook up the service that day at the women's retreat. What would seem to an outsider as out of order and chaotic was actually God rearranging a few things.

I preached, prophesied and cast out devils. I did the things that had always been done in the Bible, yet it seemed so new. I was supposed to do two workshops, but because the women wanted to stay in my workshop when they had the choice of many others, I was moved to a larger room. Announcements were rewritten, crowds were rerouted, and instructions were regiven. But in the midst of all this, everybody had smiles on their faces. The women made a beeline to my classroom. As elegant as the facility was, it could not accommodate what was occurring. Who would have thought all the women in the conference would be trying to attend one workshop when so many more were available?

As I attempted to enter my second workshop, hundreds of women crowded the door trying to get inside. As I waited in line with the crowd, a woman touched me and asked, "Have you heard about this new lady?" I responded that I had not. She began to tell me about the woman who just preached "From a Mess to a Miracle," and it finally hit me: She was talking about me. These ladies were all stirred up about me!

I could not believe anyone would be that excited

about what came out of my mouth. Pastor Joy came up behind me and yelled, "Let the speaker through." I was so green to church etiquette I was standing outside with the crowd. When I stepped into the pulpit, this time it was in a much larger room—the largest in the facility. The women were lining the wall and sitting on the floor. Many were asked to leave because the size of the crowd was breaking fire codes.

I thought my testimony "From a Mess to a Miracle" was about coming out of the world. My true testimony is about coming into the church. Everybody came out of Egypt, but many did not go into the Promised Land. The group that went in had "another spirit." Before God released Joshua into the Promised Land the most important thing He said to him was, "Moses my servant is dead!" Many try to take Moses into the Promised Land with them, and it will never work. God will use a thing for a while, and people will put their eyes on the thing and take them off of God. It is very important not to get stuck on moves of God. God will kill a move—even when He started it—and tell us to go on to something else.

Many have gotten stuck in a move of God and missed their next level. God takes us from one glory to the next. We must be watchful of the "spirit of Nuhashtan." In Numbers 21:8–9, God told Moses to have the people look on the pole with the snake wrapped around it (*Nuhashtan*), and they would be healed. From the time of Moses to Hezekiah, the people still looked to the pole for healing, even when the anointing was no longer on it. Hezekiah said that it became a brazen trifle, meaning it was not worth the material it was made of. When he tore down the high places, Nuhashtan was first to go.

God can anoint a thing and then command us to move on from it.

God can anoint a thing and then command us to move on from it. If we stay in something that God has left, the doors to witchcraft will be swung wide open. The Spirit of God leads those who are the sons of God. We must be Spirit-led in every aspect of ministry. This can be obtained only through a close relationship with the One who leads (sent) us. The medical symbol today is a pole with a snake wrapped around it. I believe this is a natural manifestation of what took place a long time ago in the spirit realm.

God is delivering His bride from the spiritual treadmill of religion. He is raising up a generation with another spirit. I believe this is an apostolic, pioneering spirit that is not afraid to go in and conquer new frontiers. People fear what they are unfamiliar with. This is one of the undercover tools of the enemy: the familiar spirit! This spirit makes its victim skeptical of things that are uncommon to them or that they cannot control. Sometimes things can become so common or familiar to us that even when it is wrong, it is still accepted.

When I was in the world, I never spent time in the church. I could not understand people who went to the club all night and arose early for Sunday morning service. My first thought about this was that it was nice to give God a little time. I called it clocking time. Before I knew Jesus as Lord, I knew Him as Savior. I accepted Him in my heart to deliver me from a life of darkness. Scripture reveals that we are translated from the kingdom of darkness into God's marvelous light.

> But ye are a chosen generation, a royal priesthood, an holy nation, a peculiar people; that ye should shew forth the praises of him who hath called you out of darkness into his marvellous light.
>
> —1 Peter 2:9

When we come out of the kingdom of darkness we accept Jesus as Savior. On the other hand, the lordship of Jesus Christ can only manifest in our lives when we come into His marvelous light.

Before I knew Jesus as Lord, I visited churches, and it always made me feel good inside. Tears would run down my face. The music would really touch me in a special way. The only problem was that I could not go to the club on Saturday night and wake up on Sunday in time to make the service. I have always purposed to put my all in whatever I did, so I had to make a choice: It was either the club or the church.

Being transformed by the renewing of our minds has a lot to do with being translated into God's marvelous light. The word *light* in 1 Peter 2:9 is *phos* in the Greek. This means "to manifest luminous, or to be full of light." Matthew 5:14 says we are supposed to be a light to the world, a city that cannot be hid. There is a counterfeit to the marvelous light in the world, a group called the *Illuminati*. They are a small group of very wealthy people who use money and influence to run the world. They are the most dangerous secret society that exists. Though they attempt to counterfeit the marvelous light, the Bible says the true marvelous light cannot be hidden.

Few people know of or understand the operations of the Illuminati, but I am mentioning them because they, along with the Masons, represent the false undercover light. We, the church, must be the true light. But we must not think that just because we come into the church that we are automatically reflecting the true light. We must make an effort to let our light shine. According to Scripture, the light in us can be made dark.

> But if thine eye be evil, thy whole body shall be full of darkness. If therefore the light that is in thee be darkness, how great is that darkness!
> —MATTHEW 6:23

We have a responsibility to the new converts who are coming after us to let our light shine. Luke 11:33 says we must let our light shine so those who come in may see the light.

We are the true light the world needs to see. The manifestation of the renewing of the mind spoken of in Romans 12 is the illumination of Jesus Christ in our lives. People do not only need to hear Jesus preached, they need to see Him lived.

Chapter II

THE HOMOSEXUAL ISSUE IN THE CHURCH

My life in the world was like movies I now see on television. The spirits I dealt with on a continual basis became very familiar to me. Because I have come out of the world and into the marvelous light of Jesus, I am very sensitive to these spirits. The only difference is that now instead of being subject to these spirits, I have power over them.

Last night I had a dream that I knew God wanted me to write about today. I was in a setting with a gathering of people who seemed to be waiting to be entertained. A man with a hairstyle like the old rock 'n roll singer Little Richard came out on the stage and began to sing the most beautiful gospel song I had ever heard. It was almost enchanting. Then all of a sudden, other men came from behind the curtain to sing behind the first man. One of the men had his clothes hanging off of his body as if he were about to strip. Two of the men began kissing each other and acting in perverse ways as the gospel song was still playing. Someone yelled from the crowd, "These are freaks!" I attempted to tell everyone what was going on, but no one was paying any attention to what I was saying. They knew what was happening, but they were mesmerized by the music.

My testimony is not one of ever participating in homosexuality, but my upbringing exposed me to the lifestyle on a level much higher than most. My father had clubs where men performed as female impersonators. I spent most of my childhood hanging out at what we called the "sissy shows." In the world I was familiar with this spirit, and I could spot a gay man with a blindfold on. When I got saved, this discerning did not leave me. As a new believer I would resist this discerning of homosexual spirits, and I always made excuses for it. My natural mind could not understand how a person could preach and sing and continue to live a gay lifestyle.

Is the world more discerning than the church?

The most difficult part was how everyone in the church could pretend that it was not there. In the world everybody knew who the sissies were. Is the world more discerning than the church? I was delivered from resisting this discernment when the son of one of my best friends was molested by her husband. He had been molesting the child for two years. My friend and I questioned the way he carried himself several times. He had many feminine characteristics, but our hearts denied the truth.

This is how many gay men I minister to were infected with the seed of homosexuality; they were molested in the church as young boys. I realize that all boys who have been homosexually molested did not get attacked in the church, but I can verify that 99 percent of the ones I minister to did. They were young boys who trusted Deacon So-and-So or Rev. Goodie-Two-Shoes. God revealed to me that in order to break the powers of this vicious cycle, we must deal with the "curse of the breeder." A breeder is a man who was molested so that the seed of homosexuality would be planted in his soul to reproduce others of his kind.

One thing I would like to emphasize is that I love homosexual men, but I hate the devils that abide in them. It is not a sickness or a birth defect. It is an assignment against the male seed by satan himself. It multiplies by contamination and transference of spirits. The manifestation reaches its peak when the victim believes the lie that has been sent his way. Homosexuality is a counterfeit and a lie. It is one of the foulest spirits I have ever dealt with personally as a deliverance minister. To imagine the smell of a homosexual spirit as it leaves a person's body would make me sick.

Scientists and psychologists have intellectually conjured up ways to explain homosexuality to the world, but God does a much better job in Romans 1.

> Because that, when they knew God, they glorified him not as God, neither were thankful; but became vain in their imaginations, and their foolish heart was darkened. Professing themselves to be wise, they became fools, and changed the glory of the uncorruptible God into an image made like to corruptible man, and to birds, and four-footed beast, and creeping things. Wherefore God also gave them up to uncleanness through the lusts of their own hearts, to dishonor their own bodies between themselves: Who changed the truth of God into a lie, and worshipped and served the creature more than the Creator, who is blessed forever. Amen. For this cause God gave them up unto vile affections: for even their women did change the natural use into that which is against nature: and likewise also the men, leaving the natural use of the woman, burned in their lust one toward another; men with men working that which is unseemly, and receiving in themselves that recompence of their error which was meet.
>
> —ROMANS 1:21–27

After reading this passage of Scripture, I can safely list these things concerning homosexuality:

1. *A person who knows God can be a homosexual.* "When they knew God, they glorified him not as God" in their lives (v. 21).

22

2. *The root spirit of homosexuality is vain imagination.* "They...became vain in their imaginations" (v. 21).

3. *Homosexuality makes the heart of the person dark.* "Their foolish heart was darkened" (v. 21).

4. *Homosexuality is an unclean spirit.* "God also gave them up unto uncleanness" (v. 24).

5. *Homosexuality is a selfish lust.* "God gave them up to uncleanness through the lusts of their own hearts" (v. 24).

6. *Homosexuality is a type of idol worship.* "They worshipped and served the creature more than the Creator" (v. 25).

7. *Homosexuality is a vile affection against nature.* "The women did change the natural use into that which is against nature" (v. 26).

8. *Homosexuality is unseemly in the eyes of God.* "Men with men working that which is unseemly" (v. 27).

9. *There is great punishment reserved for those who commit homosexual acts.* "Receiving in themselves that recompence of their error which was meet" (v. 27).

All of the above statements are undeniably verified in Romans 1:21–27, but as we take a look at verses 28–32 of the same chapter, we can get a deeper revelation of the severity of this assignment against mankind.

And even as they did not like to retain God in their knowledge, God gave them over to a reprobate mind, to do those things which are not convenient; being filled with all unrighteousness, fornication, wickedness. covetousness, maliciousness; full of envy, murder, debate, deceit, malignity; whisperers, backbiters, haters of God, despiteful, proud, boasters, inventors of evil things, disobedient to parents, without understanding, covenant-breakers, without natural affection, implacable, unmerciful: Who knowing the judgment of God, that they which commit such things are worthy of death, not only do the same, but have pleasure in them that do them.

The Amplified Bible states verse 32 this way:

Though they are fully aware of God's righteous decree that those who do such things deserve to die, they not only do them themselves but approve and applaud others who practice them.

The Bible says we should judge a tree by the fruit it bears. Review the above list of fruit in a homosexual person's life. I can verify that all of these spirits dominate the lives of those living the gay lifestyle. Here are a few more truths about homosexuality based on this passage of Scripture.

10. *The homosexual spirit is a strongman that has many other spirits working with it* (see vv. 29–31).

11. *Homosexuality is a road to reprobation* (see v. 28).

24

12. *Most homosexuals are afraid to come out of the closet and cursed to live a lifestyle of inconvenience* (see v. 28).

13. *Most homosexuals are fully aware that their lifestyle is sinful* (see v. 32).

Let us review. When the word of the Lord states that the spirit of homosexuality makes mankind (male and female) "dishonor their own bodies between themselves" (Rom. 1:24), it is important to refer to the Greek interpretation. The word *themselves* is pronounced *heh-ow-too*. This word means "to love your own body or to be conceited." This is what I call the curse of Narcissus. He was a Greek god who fell in love with his reflection in the water. Homosexuality is a type of self love or love of self. It is when a person is sexually attracted to his or her own body. In other words, a body of the opposite sex does not turn them on; they only desire someone "just like their own selves."

Whatever is in the root will feed the tree.

Masturbation opens a door to homosexuality. Whatever is in the root will feed the tree. It takes vain imagination to masturbate, and vain imagination is the root spirit of homosexuality. Masturbation is a type of self-sex in the natural, though the person is never alone in the spirit. Incubus and Succubus (sexual demons) lie in waiting for masturbating victims to enter their body and help with the sex act. In studying the occult, perverted sex acts have always been a climax to sacrifices unto satan. Whenever semen is released in ways that God has not ordained, it is a sacrifice unto satan. This is why lesbian and homosexual acts are so popular in temple worship.

In Genesis 38:9, the Bible states that Onan spilled his seed to the ground to avoid impregnating his wife, Tamar. That word *spilled* in the Hebrew is *shâchath*, and it means "to waste or corrupt the seed." When seed is released in acts such as fornication, masturbation and homosexuality, it becomes corrupt in the eyes of God. Earlier, we read that homosexuality is "unseemly" in the eyes of the Lord. The Greek interpretation for *unseemly* is "to be indecent and shameful."

It is my prayer that homosexuals from around the world—in the church and outside of the church—will read this message and hear. There is a cry in the spirit from men and women who want to be released from this bondage. In the church especially, homosexuality has become a familiar spirit. We look at it and wink, but God is not winking. He loves homosexuals and wants them to be set free. This sin is a mockery to God. I see it as a Goliath that is standing in the church saying, "Does anyone have enough power to come up against me?" All of Israel sat still as the giant mocked the Most High God. It is time to shut Goliath's mouth, and the only way to shut his mouth is to make him fall—and the only way to do that is to aim at his head.

When we deal with the homosexuality in the pulpits and on the pianos, the entire body will be open for deliverance. It is time out for preachers preaching against homosexuality and not being able to do anything about it. I make this statement with no offensive intention. If a person cannot cast out a homosexual spirit, there is no use in yelling about it. David addressed Goliath verbally, but he had five smooth stones to back his words up. I believe these stones represented the five-fold ministry, which God gave to the church "for the perfecting of the saints . . . till we all come in the unity of faith" (Ephesians 4:12–13). This refers to the maturity of the church and our coming together toward one faith. Without unity, we cannot obtain this maturity.

The homosexual spirit is an antichrist spirit, and it will never unite with the purpose of God. I believe the closets in the church are about to be cleaned out. Homosexuality is about to be exposed and dealt with. Out of this move of God will come a group with "another spirit." They will have a "well able" spirit. Because they have been forgiven much, they will love much. What the devil has meant for evil will be thrown back into his face to haunt him. Because the devil has used homosexuals as breeders to infiltrate and contaminate the male seed, God will turn it around and use them to breed deliverance for others to come out of the same darkness they once knew.

There are two types of homosexual breeders in the church:

1. The people who consciously or unconsciously support homosexuality by not addressing the issue. Romans 1:32 says there is even a group that approves and applauds

this lifestyle. (See the Amplified Bible.)

2. The molesters and seed droppers who transfer spirits in various ways.

As God has delivered me out of the world "against all odds," He has delivered me into the church, a transition that can only be described as coming "from a mess to a miracle." I have a word of encouragement to homosexuals who hang out in the church: "Come all the way in!" I know you are miserable, but you are reaping the fruit of an ancient curse. Homosexuality is a generational curse that started with the iniquities of God's people a long time ago. It is also a type of death spirit that walks hand in hand with suicide and depression. Scripture describes homosexuals as "suffering in their own bodies and personalities." (See Romans 1:27, AMP.) The Bible also says those who participate in homosexuality deserve to die:

> Who knowing the judgment of God, that they which commit such things are worthy of death, not only do the same, but have pleasure in them that do them.
> —ROMANS 1:32

Though God loves homosexuals, the enemy seeks to steal, kill and destroy. He knows that those who commit these acts will reap the repercussion, which is death.

I happen to believe that if a person bound by the spirit of homosexuality had someone they could trust (who walked in power over this unclean spirit), they would run to deliverance. If you are reading this book and struggling with this spirit, please pray this prayer with me:

PRAYER OF REPENTANCE FOR DELIVERANCE FROM HOMOSEXUALITY

Father God, in the name of Jesus, I repent of my sins and repent of the generational iniquities of my forefathers to the fourth generation. I renounce the lie. I lay down this lifestyle and pick up **zoe** *life. I renounce the shame; I renounce the perverseness of my thoughts and my ways. I plead the blood of Jesus over my mind and command the stronghold over my life to come down. I take authority over the vain imaginations that have gripped my soul, and I lead them captive into the obedience of Christ. I command the hook of pride and the strongman of leviathan, who watches over every high thing, to be disconnected. Satan, I pull your power plug in my life, and I tap into the fullness of Christ Jesus. Jesus, I renounce the strongman of lust and perversion. Forgive me of my sins. Come into my heart and be Lord! Lord, send someone in my life whom I can trust to minister to me. You are my deliverer and my salvation, and I thank You for the person You will use for me to agree with in the earthly realm. Thank You, Jesus. Amen!*

For the everyday person, transition from the kingdom of darkness to the church is not an easy process. Can you imagine what it is like for a homosexual to accept Jesus as Lord and Savior and then find a church home that can deal with his or her issues? Just like the woman with the issue of blood, many do not want to touch things like this. It was all right for this woman to have her issue as long as she did not bring it to the public eye. This is a fear that we must be delivered from in the church—manifestation. The church does not mind people getting healed or delivered as long as they do not manifest before the people.

Whenever you allow one spirit to hang around, he will soon be accompanied by many more.

Sometimes manifestations can be ugly. Jesus asked the spirits in the demoniac, "What is your name?" The demons in the man responded, "My name is legion for we are many." This scripture should teach us a great lesson. In dealing with one devil, there will always be many more spirits to address. Satan has a kingdom, and we are actually confronting alliances and ranks of dark forces. The spirit said that his name was legion. This defines a regiment of devils. We are in a war, and there are platoons, battalions and even armies of unclean spirits on assignment against the church. The demons were first referred to as singular and then plural. Why? Because whenever you allow one spirit to hang around, he will soon be accompanied by many more.

Devils never work alone.

Devils never work alone. Revelation 18:1 speaks of how Babylon had fallen and became the habitation of devils, a holding cage for every kind of foul spirit. The reason given for this formation of devils is that the nations drunk of the wine, wrath and fornication of the whore of Babylon.

I began this book talking about transformation vs. conformity to the likeness of Christ. This is a bottom-line message with no hidden agendas between the lines. Either we are transformed into that which is acceptable to God, or we will be transformed into the image of what pleases satan. If we are not totally translated into the marvelous light of Jesus Christ, the light that it is in us will become darkness. Luke 11:33 says that no man who has lit a candle will hide it in a secret place; he will leave it out so that "they that come in may see the light." The greatest evangelistic tool we have is to let our lights shine. Evangelism is not only winning the lost, but also maintaining the souls that have already come in.

Luke said the ones who have come in must see the light. He expounded in Luke 11:34, saying the light of the body is the eye. The word *eye* in the Greek is *opthalmos*, and it means "vision" or "that which can be seen." This word is related to the English word *optical* or *optometry*, all relating to the eye. *Opthalmos* comes out of the Greek word *optanomai*, which means "to watch or observe." Luke said that if the eye is evil the whole body is full of darkness. When he warns us to take heed that the light in us be not darkness, could he have been referring to our influence on "them that come in"?

New converts need to see the light in us. Before our light can shine in the world, it must shine within the church. This is where "the power that is in us" spoken of in Ephesians 3:20 must manifest. Ephesians 3:16–19 talks about the rich treasury of Christ's glory that strengthens and reinforces our inner man. This reference also addresses being rooted and grounded in love and knowing the love of Christ, which passes knowledge.

Satan is the author of confusion and the father of lies. When we are born again, the enemy's job is to make sure we are the most miserable Christians in the earth. Coming out of Egypt represented a type of new birth and being released from the bondage of the enemy. After the children of Israel came into the wilderness, the enemy painted every picture he could to put them in a state of discontent so they would complain. The enemy wants us to consider what we have come out of as a better state of life. There are many challenges in the Christian life, but God warned us in His Word that there would be. We need mentors with victory in their lives and compassion in their hearts to mentor a generation that will not waste time complaining.

Paul told the church at Galatia to hold on to their liberty so that they would not be entangled with the yoke of bondage again. Then he began to address the issue of religion and tradition. The worst thing we could ever do to a person is to bring them out of the world and introduce them to a system of tradition and religion. It is just another vicious cycle that is designed to push them back into the world. When I walked through the doors of the church the demon of religion addressed me face to face. This spirit told me that if its friends could not torment me in the world, it would torment me in the church. The spirit was too stupid to know that my mind was made up; I was not going back.

I had to come to grips with the fact that if I did not torment devils, they would torment me. I have a good friend who often says, "I discipline devils." That is such a powerful phrase because the Word says demonic spirits are subject to us and not the opposite. I have to remind people all the time that I do not look for devils; they are looking for me. I do not have a problem when I run into devils; they have a problem when they run into me. When Jesus stepped into the synagogue (church), the devils cried out, "Lord, what do You have to do with us?" To paraphrase this, the devils were saying, "Lord, what are You doing in the church?" These same devils had been there all the time. We are about to walk into a season when the devils will not come to our churches and sit comfortably. The strength of the message God has given me is that we cannot deal with the darkness that is around us until we deal with the darkness that is inside of us.

When the Greater One takes His place as Lord on

the thrones inside of us, revival as our minds cannot fathom will be released. The anointing of God will rush through the sanctuaries and command mass deliverance. When the anointing came in, the devils manifested, which means "to come out of darkness." To manifest is to make clear that which was once obscure. It is timeout for swinging at shadows and always feeling like we are being followed around. If we have enemies, we ought to know who they are.

In biblical times, God named the enemies of His people. For example, He referenced the Hittites, Amorites and Jebusites as enemies of the children of Israel. If I run into a snake that is bold enough to lift its head, I take pleasure in cutting it off. Many are the afflictions of the righteous, but God delivers us from them all.

When we recognize a thief, we can make him give back what was stolen seven times.

My comfort is in Nahum 1:9, which says that no affliction shall come upon us a second time. The children of Israel wandered around in the same vicious cycle for forty years. Receiving the revelation of Nahum 1:9 takes us into the benefit Proverbs 6:31. When we recognize a thief, we can make him give back what was stolen seven times.

But if he be found, he shall restore sevenfold; he

shall give all the substance of his house.

—PROVERBS 6:31

I am in the place in my life where I have received the revelation that this is not my season to be robbed. I am in the season of my life where devils have to pay for all I have been through in my past. If I waste time going through the same things over and over, I will not be in place to receive the restoration of what has already been stolen from me. I make a legal proclamation in the spirit that my head is covered by Nahum 1:9, and I stand on Proverbs 6:31. There are many challenges as we press toward the high calling of God, but I would rather be a doorkeeper in the house of the Lord than to dwell in the tent of the wicked.

Chapter III

THE SPIRIT OF POVERTY

The Bible says we are to be witnesses in all the earth. It is very important that we not only tell people about Jesus, but also live lives that testify of His goodness. No one witnessed to me about Jesus when I was in the world. I really do not remember anyone aggressively approaching me about salvation. I can count on my hands when a Christian mildly mentioned church, Jesus or anything to do with the gospel. My mentality was so far from God that for a person to minister to me they could not approach me from a religious standpoint.

Most of the people I came in contact with who

claimed to be saved painted a picture of salvation that was very undesirable to me. I will never forget Mrs. Christina. She lived five houses down from me when I was in the military at Fort Stewart, Georgia. She was a Christian woman who always told me about how she had Jesus, though she never attempted to tell me how I could get Him. I remember how she always had a funny smell. Her living conditions were not the best, and she was always in desperate need of simple necessities. Many times she would sadly tell me that she and her children would have to go to bed without dinner. She had a husband who lived in the house, but she never mentioned him in our conversations.

I would often wonder why this woman was around me. I had strong philosophies about life when I was in the world. One of them was that I did not waste my time with people I did not have anything in common with. I would literally ask people questions like, "Do you get high?"; "Do you party?"; or, "We have nothing in common, so why are we hanging out?" I felt as if people who did not do these types of things had no life. This was the best way I could relate to the "good life."

My goal in life was to have money and to be famous. I had no hope of ever becoming famous on my own, so my plan was to marry a famous man. My exposure to the athletic world led me to believe that I would find a husband who would sweep me off my feet and move me to Hollywood. My dreams were crushed when the man that I met swept me off my feet and moved me to the mental institution. When I signed up for the military, so many failed plans haunted me that I decided it was better not to plan at all.

The Spirit of Poverty

When Mrs. Christina sat at my kitchen counter telling me about her hard times, I was in a transition in my life. I was at a place where I felt as if I could not fight anymore. Fighting had always been the answer for me, but my right hook was getting weak. I just wanted to be normal. Having been in the spotlight all my life was finally taking a toll on my heart, and I was coming to the realization that something or someone bigger than me had an influence over my life. I needed something, and I did not know what it was. It was something like an itch that wouldn't go away.

As I looked into Mrs. Christina's eyes, her need seemed so deep. What she did not realize was that my need was deeper than hers. My need was spiritual, and her need was physical. She had Jesus, and I did not have a clue about Him. The sad thing was that the one who was supposed to have Him did not have enough of Him to give me. As I think back, I remember that she would pause every now and then in the midst of her bad luck stories and religiously shout "Hallelujah!," "Praise God," or "Thank You, Jesus!" I could not tell which one of us was in the worst condition. I was a heathen and far from knowing Jesus at all. But Mrs. Christina only knew Him from a religious standpoint and had no concept of Jesus as her Deliverer and Provider.

My natural instincts told me that if she served a God who was so powerful and loved her so much, He would not allow her family to starve every night. Mrs. Christina would quote the few scriptures she had memorized, but something on the inside of me knew she had no idea what she was saying. My compassion for her became so great because I could not imagine my babies being continually hungry. She had a new house, just as I did, but roaches would crawl out of the refrigerator. Her struggle was so strong, and I did not have any answers for her.

At least once a week I cleaned out my refrigerator and gave Mrs. Christina and her family all the food I could spare. They lived in a house built by the government, so their mortgage was little or nothing. Even still, the lights were often cut off, and the furniture had that same odor I smelled in Mrs. Christina's clothes. I am sure Mrs. Christina did not know it, but that scent is related to the spirit of poverty.

Demons are referred to as foul spirits in the Bible. The definition of *foul* is "to be putrid, offensive and impure." Demons are also called unclean. Today I can detect the same smell of Mrs. Christina's house in many homes. My husband and I both agree that it is a distinct odor that is always accompanied with poverty and lack. This stench is definitely spiritual because no matter how much the person cleans, the smell is still there. There is also a dark gray film that lurks in the air over these homes.

Some have been offended when I tried to minister to them in this area. The spirit of poverty has crucial elements that a person does not need a spiritual gift to detect. In the neighborhoods I grew up in, it is common to live with roaches. Christians do not have to call down fire or pray in tongues to get rid of them. Just call the exterminator on a frequent basis. I know from experience that the devil will trick a person's mind to make him think living in a roach-infested house is normal.

My husband comes from a living environment that was far worse than mine. He has told me stories of how roaches would eat his naval cord out when he was a baby. My ministry has been very effective in what we call the "gutter most," but sometimes my messages have to get down and dirty. For example, I remember hearing the Holy Ghost so clearly one day saying, "There are demons in the dirt!" When I started preaching messages on spiritually and physically cleaning house, a few people got offended—especially when I started messing with their pet roaches. They felt like I was picking on them in an area that they could not help. I understood where they were because, as the saying goes, I had been there and done that, too! But as an apostle of God it was my responsibility to let them know that they did not have to stay where they were. I thank God that those who had ears heard what God was saying and are now living in houses that are not just anointed but bug-free.

"There are demons in the dirt!"

Most people who have lived in ghetto environments and survived welfare were never taught basic principles of living. I believe that this is the mentoring aspect of evangelism. Sometimes for the full process of the renewing of the mind to kick in we have to get involved with the private lives of people. We run a tight ship at Spoken Word that many would not understand. I believe ministers of the gospel should have basic provisions, such as money to put gas in their cars. I have rebuked many ministers who were trying to travel on the road while leaving their children home with no food in the refrigerator. There is a spirit that will make you settle for less. I know the signs, and it all adds up to what I call "poverty complacency." People get used to empty refrigerators, having milk once a week or having to get gas money from the people they are picking up for church. These things should be dealt with immediately. Not only are they unacceptable, but also they are spiritual assignments that will keep people from fulfilling God's vision for their lives.

Staying on top of everyday issues such as maintaining a good driver's license, having car insurance and changing the oil in their cars is not common in the lives of many of the people I deal with. No one ever took the time to teach them that these are priorities in life. They are used to hustling, borrowing money and never paying it back or hanging out with you every day and letting you buy their lunch with no conviction in their hearts about ever returning the favor.

In the first chapter I talked about transformation and transition. When people conform to what they have always been exposed to, their opportunity for transformation is destroyed. Without transformation of the mind, there will be no transition to the next level. Numbers 14:24 says Caleb and Joshua had "another spirit," one different from the others wandering in the wilderness. The word *spirit* in this passage is *ruwach*. One of the meanings of this Hebrew word is "mind." Joshua and Caleb did not focus on what they were up against in life. They said, "Not only are we able, but we are *well* able!" They went forward to possess what God had promised them.

The other folk in the wilderness had no hope of transition. Just like Mrs. Christina, they came out of darkness (Egypt), but they never entered the marvelous light (the land of milk and honey). After God delivers us from whatever our Egypt was—and by the way, we all have an Egypt!—we must get a new attitude to enter into the fullness of salvation.

The word *salvation* means more than coming to church every week busted, disgusted and can't even be trusted. It is *soteria* in the Greek, and it means "welfare, safety, deliverance and health." Please do not misinterpret my message. I understand that people will have challenges in life, but we must consider the vicious cycle of the python of poverty. It is consistent and usually has a pattern that can be easily detected. This python spirit slowly squeezes the provision out of a person's life. It will allow much to go out and nothing to come in. A sure sign of this spirit is a lot of bills with no provision to pay them. A clear sign is when the bills are getting higher and the money is getting lower. There are several financial curses that should be recognized and renounced. Let us review them:

1. **The curse of Cain.** Proverbs 3:9 says we should honor the Lord with all of our substance and the firstfruit of all our increase. The Word of the Lord goes on to say that if we obey this statute, God will fill our barns with plenty. Cain was cursed to the land of Nod, which means "the land of nothing." When we try to hold back on God, we end up

with nothing.

2. **The curse of Malachi.** Malachi 3:10 tells us to bring all the tithes into the storehouse. When we obey this principle, God promises to open the windows of heaven over our heads. He also promises to rebuke the hand of the devourer on our behalf. Many are plagued with curses because they do not honor God in their tithes and offerings. They are holy unto God. Some make the mistake of not releasing their tithes in their minds. They mentally follow the money to the offering room, to the banks and even the board meeting to worry about how it is spent.

When we try to hold back on God, we end up with nothing.

Scripturally speaking, it is not the responsibility of the individual who is tithing to decide how the money is spent in the house of God. The word *holy* means "separated unto God." We do not tithe properly until we give it as unto the Lord and separate from it in our minds.

For as he thinketh in his heart, so is he.
—PROVERBS 23:7

Our tithing is not pleasing unto the Lord until we have the right attitude about it.

3. **The curse of Haggai.** Let's take a look at
   the fruits of this curse:

   ↜ You expected much but little came in.

   ↜ When you brought the little that came in
     home, it was blown away.

   ↜ The heaven over you was stayed with dew.

   ↜ The earth was stayed from her fruit.

   ↜ A drought was called upon the land.

   ↜ A drought was called upon the corn, new
     wine, oil, produce of the ground, men,
     cattle and labor of men's hands.

What could these people have done to upset God
like this? Haggai 1:9 reveals that God was angry because
His house was wasted. Every man was running to his
own house. Verse 4 says the people sat in their own
sealed houses while the house of God lay in ruins. The
people said that it was not time for the Lord's house to
be rebuilt, but they took care of the needs of their own
houses instead.

4. **The generational curse of poverty.** Exodus
   20:5 explains how the iniquities of the fathers
   go back as far as four generations. The Bible
   declares that if the fathers do not hearken to
   the voice of the Lord to do His commandments, poverty is one of the curses that shall
   be a sign upon their seed.

And they shall be upon thee for a sign and for a

wonder, and upon thy seed for ever.

—Deuteronomy 28:46

5. **The curse of Ananias and Sapphira.** The root of the sin committed by Ananias and Sapphira is made clear in the Book of Ecclesiastes. It says, "Better is it that thou shouldest not vow, than that thou shouldest vow and not pay" (Eccles. 5:5). They put their property up for sale using church advertisement. After making a vow to God, they refused to give the proceeds to the church. They became "spiritual jack men," and they did it in the face of God.

It would have been better for the Internal Revenue Service to come and deal with them, but theirs was a much more horrible fate. It was a time of great revival. The people were laying their offerings at the feet of the apostles, while Ananias and Sapphira robbed God. This was one time the sister should not have submitted. She received the same punishment as her husband. Peter exposed their sin as keeping back a "part" of the profit and lying to the Holy Ghost.

As a preacher from the inner city and an apostle to the nations, the vision of God on the inside of me will not rest until the people around me are blessed. Since the time of Mrs. Christina, I've had a hard time being successful in life and hanging around people with failing spirits. I realize that everyone does not desire to succeed in life. Despite this, it is my purpose to push all who want to succeed out of the bands of the wickedness of poverty. I can only do this with the help of the Lord. I feel that my ministry is not fulfilling the vision of Christ unless the lives of the people around me change for the better. Besides all that, it is a sin to live below the standard that God has given us.

The military provides for the welfare of the soldiers so their families can be taken care of at all times. The spirit of "need" will distract any good soldier from doing an excellent job. The military does not take it kindly when they provide a check on the first of the month and the creditors are calling on the second of the month. I believe God is the same way. Jesus died so that we would not have to suffer from spirits of poverty and lack. When He came to set the captives free, He took the chains off of our bank accounts and unlocked our minds concerning it. *Selah!* (Pause and think on that.)

I have seen homosexuals, crack addicts and people with tragic situations miraculously set free. But I get the greatest joy out of seeing a poverty-stricken person transitioned into the financial promises of God. There is a young woman in my church who is a single mother with five children. When she came to the ministry she was making $123 every two weeks. This was her only income. She had been to jail and homeless, and her children had been incarcerated.

She had attempted suicide several times a year, but today I can honestly testify that the curse is broken. Over seven months her income has increased to $3,000 per month, and she has the joy of the Lord. Her testimony is that she does not have to hold her head down anymore. She can look people in the face now. She has a new attitude. Her entire mind-set about herself and her provision has changed. Poverty is a spirit of the mind; it is a mentality. It has to hit the soul before it can ever touch your purse. This young woman's life has changed, and there is a new glow on her face. She even looks prettier than before. Poverty is an ugly spirit.

The keys to freedom from poverty are available to everyone. The church doesn't need more Mrs. Christinas to make Jesus seem unconcerned about one's physical condition. Walk in victory over the spirit of lack and allow God to bring a transformation that takes you to the next level.

Chapter IV

DISCERNING
OF SPIRITS

The discerning of spirits may be one of the most misunderstood and overlooked gifts in operation in the body. God has given both leadership and operational gifts to the church. The leadership gifts identify the people ordained by God to operate in the five-fold ministry outlined in Ephesians 4:11.

> And he gave some, apostles; and some, prophets; and some, evangelists; and some, pastors and teachers.
>
> —EPHESIANS 4:11

The gifts in 1 Corinthians 12 chart the operation of

God's Spirit through His people in the church.

I believe that as the end-time church, we are about to walk in a better understanding of the offices and functions of the gifts of the spirit. The word *discerning* is *diakrisis* in the Greek, and it is defined as "judicial estimation." It means to become an accurate judge of what is going on in the spirit realm. This word is derived out of the Greek word *diakrino*, which means "to be able to differentiate or to tell the difference." It also means the gift to thoroughly separate. I would like to note three different types of discerning of spirits that God has given me to expound upon. Please note that I am not saying these are the only kinds of discerning of spirits; these are the ones that God has revealed to me.

1. Priestly discerning of spirits.

This kind of discerning of spirits has been designated to those who walk in the priestly anointing. Leviticus 10:10 teaches that it is the responsibility of the priest to differentiate between holy and unholy, clean and unclean. The Amplified Bible says the priest should teach the difference between what is secular and what is holy. God would not give this responsibility to leaders without endowing them with the discernment to do it.

The priest should teach the difference between what is secular and what is holy.

Discerning of Spirits

The word *difference* is pronounced *baw-dal* in the Hebrew, and it means "to discern, separate or utterly divide asunder." Bishops, pastors and other ministry gifts who shepherd over the souls of men are held accountable to this principle. God declares that His people perish for a lack of knowledge.

> My people are destroyed for lack of knowledge: because thou hast rejected knowledge, I will also reject thee, that thou shalt be no priest to me: seeing thou hast forgotten the law of thy God, I will also forget thy children.
>
> —HOSEA 4:6

The people cannot obey what they do not know. I remember when I used to attend services and the gifts of the Spirit would begin to flow. I thanked God that I was not the one responsible to keep the order of the house. What if someone gave a word that was not from the Lord? How would anyone know? I would tremble and think, *What an awesome responsibility.*

Later as I became a pastor of a congregation, I found out how faithful God really is to help me shoulder this responsibility. He would never put you in a position and leave you hanging. I have had to rebuke many people who were out of order in a worship service, but when you are tapped into the vein of God, you just flow. How do you know what is going on in the spirit? I don't have a formula; you just know.

It is very important that pastors and leaders understand the authority of the set man. We can compare the apostle, pastor or bishop of the house to Michael Jordan on the basketball court. When the heat is on, give the ball to Mike. He will know what to do with it because he is the set man. In a full-court press, he does not have time to figure the play out. The instincts of the game drive him. He may miss a few shots (we all fall short of the glory), but he is known for his accuracy on the court. You cannot go to seminary to learn how to flow in a congregational setting when the gifts are operating. Walking in priestly discernment requires a combination of: (1) appointment by God to a position; (2) experience (you learn by doing it); (3) understanding and walking in your authority; and (4) total submission to the Holy Spirit and renunciation of the natural man who is the mind of the flesh.

2. The gift of discerning of spirits.

This gift is given to whomever the Lord chooses to give it to. I personally have witnessed children as young as three and four walking heavily in the gift of discerning of spirits. God revealed to me that babies who scream and cry uncontrollably when certain people come around are sometimes discerning unclean spirits on the person. This is not always the case, because it may be that evil spirits are tormenting the baby and the anointing on the person's life is stirring up these spirits.

Leaders need to learn more about this gift so they can train and nurture people in the congregation who are being used of God in this area. With covering, understanding and nurturing, people with this gift can truly be a blessing. On the other hand, people with this gift who use it out of control can shut the doors of the church. The spirit realm is very real, and there are two forces operating in it.

I thank God that He has gifted people in the body to discern spirits, but this gift must be used with humility and submission. A person with the gift of discerning spirits must be submitted to apostolic authority. They must be mentored to learn about this gift and how to use it. Even after training and exposure, a person with this spiritual endowment must have a high level of faith. This is a gift that prompts the person to literally grow up in it. As the person begins to gain confidence in what he sees in the spirit and walks in it, he will learn how to ignore the voices that are assigned against this gift.

A person with the gift of discerning spirits must be submitted to apostolic authority.

Some of the strongmen that are specifically assigned to oppose this gift are:

1. **Rabshakeh (2 Kings 18:19).** This spirit talks the people of God out of what He has shown them. Rabshakeh asked Hezekiah, "In what confidence do you trust in your God?" (AMP). This spirit also tries to get the person to believe that the words they have from the Lord are in vain. This is a type of whispering spirit. It whispers to the mind through thoughts of false counsel.

2. **Cockatrice (Isaiah 14:29).** This is a mind-blinding spirit. The cockatrice is a

mythological creature that is said to have a deadly glance. The assignment of the cockatrice is to release spirits of error and confusion. The word *cockatrice* is pronounced *tsif-o-nee* in the Hebrew, and it refers to "a hissing adder or outcast thing." The manifestation of this spirit is a hissing tongue that is a result of what has been seen. This spirit must be bound and renounced. It is assigned against every person with the gift of discerning of spirits. The goal of this assignment is to get the person to become critical of what they have discerned and to obtain a hissing, viperous tongue. I have seen this spirit manifest itself in the eye and the tongue of the person while going through deliverance.

3. **Sanballat and Tobiah (Nehemiah 4:1).** This spirit attacks those who build in the spirit. People who properly operate in the gift of discerning of spirits are builders in the spirit. The devil does not care about ministries that build physical edifices because they are not a threat to him. The fruit of a ministry that builds in the spirit is that it has compassion for the welfare of the people. Discerning of spirits is not a gift to display how anointed people are or how well they see in the spirit realm. Psychics can see in the spirit very well. This gift is to exhort, build, warn and protect the body. It is for the welfare of the people.

Nehemiah 2:10 shows us that when the enemies of God heard that the man of God was not only trying to build a work, but seeking the welfare of the people, it grieved them exceedingly. When they heard that the work of the Lord was prospering, they attacked it with reproach. In Nehemiah 4:2 they questioned the work of God. They asked questions such as: "Who do these feeble Christians think they are?" "Will they finish the work?" "Are they willing to make the sacrifice that it will take?" "What makes them think they can revive the rubbish we have burned?"

They even mocked the work questioning its stability. They said, "If a fox walks across it, it will fall." A fox is known for its light steps, so they were essentially saying the work would not stand. Nehemiah prayed a very interesting prayer. He prayed that the reproach they sent toward the work would be reversed upon their own heads. He justified his prayer based on the fact that they had provoked God.

3. Discerning of spirits for the born-again believer.

I believe the Bible supports the fact that every believer has a certain level of discernment given to him or her. Romans 8 says the sons and daughters of God are led by His Spirit. First Corinthians 2:15 tells us that he who is spiritual judges, or discerns, all things. First John 4:1 says that as believers we must try the spirits to judge whether they are of God or not. The word *try* in this scripture is *dokimazo*, and it means "to examine and discern."

It is urgent in the last days that leaders do not try to

keep their congregation in spiritual cradles. It is timeout for pastors who have to rock their members to sleep every time they cry. The five-fold ministry gifts are for the perfecting of the saints. This word *perfecting* means "maturing." In reviewing Hebrews 5:13–14, it is important to note that the maturing of the flock is a must in the last days: "For every one that useth milk is unskillful in the word of righteousness: for he is a babe. But strong meat belongeth to them that are of full age, even those who *by reason of use have their senses exercised to discern both good and evil*" (emphasis added).

This scripture clearly tells us that there are born-again believers who have: (1) matured in the area of discerning spirits by reason of use; and (2) exercised to discern both good and evil.

The opposite of discerning is being dull of hearing.

The opposite of discerning is being dull of hearing. Hebrews 5:11 says there are many things to be taught to the general body, but they are difficult to say because the people have become dull in their hearing. The word *dull* is pronounced *no-thros* in the Greek. It means "to be lazy, sluggish or slow to hear." In other words, the people heard what was convenient for them to hear. They did not hear what took them out of their comfort zones.

In the Book of Judges, God told Gideon to speak to the ears of the people. The word *ears* in this passage is *ozen* in the Hebrew. It means to have ears that weigh the benefits, or to have ears like a pair of scales. This term relates to the earlier term *no-thros*, which means "to hear what is convenient or beneficial." God said that we must "work out" our salvation with fear and trembling.

> Wherefore, my beloved, as ye have always obeyed, not as in my presence only, but now much more in my absence, work out your own salvation with fear and trembling.
>
> —PHILIPPIANS 2:12

Working out in the natural serves two purposes: to lose any excess weight, and to build or strengthen what is left so that it will be firm and strong.

The Bible declares that praying in the spirit is a workout. It builds up our most holy faith.

> But ye, beloved, building up yourselves on your most holy faith, praying in the Holy Ghost.
>
> —JUDE 1:20

We must partake in spiritual workouts so we will not be overweight concerning the things of God. We exercise our spiritual discerners by reason of use. The Book of Revelation repeatedly says, "He that hath an ear, let him hear what the Spirit saith unto the churches." The word *ear* is *ooce* in the Greek, which is interpreted as "a mental ear" or mind to hear what God is saying.

Paul touched on this issue in 1 Corinthians when he told the church at Corinth he had not come to them with enticing words of man's wisdom. He emphasized that he was teaching by the Holy Ghost, comparing spiritual things to spiritual things. In doing this he identified the enemy that would hinder the true discernment concerning the things of God--"the natural man." In the occult world this is a term for a believer who walks by what he sees instead of by faith in God. Willing participants in occult activity believe they can easily curse a "natural man."

Paul said the natural man would not receive the things of the spirit because they are foolishness to him. He goes on to say the natural man cannot know the deeper things of God because they are spiritually discerned. The curse of the natural man is the fruit of religion. It has a form of godliness, but it denies the power thereof.

> Having a form of godliness, but denying the power thereof: from such turn away.
> —2 TIMOTHY 3:5

There are so many things religious people do not believe in that are scriptural. They deny the power of things such as women in ministry, speaking in tongues, casting out devils and more. They are distracted by and drawn to things that concern the outer appearance. Apparel and programs become the agenda of their everyday worship, and there is no spirit or truth in any of it.

The sad part is that there are demons behind these religious acts. The religious spirit is the strongest spirit I have warred against as a believer. This is a devil that you will waste your time trying to cast out if you do not deal with its essence. The essence of the religious spirit is a garment of bondage or a cloak of deception that must be removed before true deliverance can take place. There are principalities that rule over every religious network, and Scripture proves this easily. Let us take a look at 1 Corinthians 2:7–8: "But we speak the wisdom of God in a mystery, even the hidden wisdom, which God ordained before the world unto our glory: which none of the princes of this world knew: for had they known it, they would not have crucified the Lord of glory."

To clarify my point, I must note that the word *princes* is related to the word *principality* in the Greek. We know that physical people killed Jesus. It is also safe to say religious people called for His execution. Despite this, the Bible makes reference to higher powers than the people who killed Jesus. Ephesians 2 talks about the prince of the power of the air that rules over the children of disobedience. The people carried out the orders, but the orders were written in the second heaven. The devil used the tool of religion to kill the Lord of glory. The good thing about this scripture is that even though the devil's plan was completed, he had no understanding of what he was doing.

The Bible says if he had known what he was doing, he would not have done it. Glory to God! Paul mentioned the mystery of the hidden wisdom. God ordained this wisdom before the world was created for our glory. This scripture is speaking specifically about "our glory" as a believer. Many believers do not know that they have a glory, but Colossians 1:27 says this glory is Christ in us, the hope of glory. That is the one thing the devil and his crew cannot counterfeit, "Christ in us." Because the dark side does not have this benefit, their knowledge of the mysteries of God is null and void. As believers we must take advantage of the Christ in us.

Sharpening your discerner requires spiritual discipline.

If you are a believer and you feel like you have not been taking advantage of your spiritual discernment, it is not too late. Sharpening your discerner requires spiritual discipline, first of all. As with working out in the natural, the most difficult part of the regimen is developing the discipline to stick to it. As you get started, I suggest you first ask yourself, "Am I a religious person?" If you are not sure, here are some indicators of religion:

1. You are a regimented person; any change in your schedule upsets you in an unusual way.

2. Your prayers are repetitive, and you often run out of things to pray as soon as you start praying.

3. You find yourself being very judgmental of how things appear, and what people think is an obsession to you.

4. You are very comfortable with how things have always been and have guarded yourself against any move of God that you are not familiar with.

5. You have difficulty obeying God when you know He has spoken because what He has told you to do does not make sense.

These indicators are not written in stone to be a guideline for the religious spirit. Based on the experiences I have had with this spirit, if you exhibit three of these five behaviors I would pray this prayer:

Father God, in the name of Jesus, I renounce every form of godliness that would cause me to deny the essence of God's true power. I renounce any zeal that I have obtained in God that is not according to true knowledge. I renounce the obsession of worrying about what people think. I refuse to be a "people pleaser," and I break loose from the paradigms of the expectations of others.

I pull down every guard I have built around my mind that causes me to reject legitimate moves of God because of a lack of familiarity. I renounce my way and receive the way of Christ. Father, forgive me for being judgmental of things and people I do not understand. I release the people I have held in contempt in the spirit because of my set ways.

I renounce religious regimen and declare that I am a child of God and will be led by the Spirit of God. I separate myself from the rudiments of men, man's religion, vain religion (James 1:26) and antichrist religions that persecute the church of God (Gal. 1:12). I commit to come

*out of the comfort zone of accepting only things
I can easily understand. I renounce the natural
man (1 Corinthians 2:14). I believe and receive
the fact that my spiritual discerner is being
sharpened as I speak! I am not dull of hearing
from the Lord, and I have an eye in the spirit to
see the vision God is revealing to me.*

*Lord Jesus, I thank You that I am walking in the
spirit of pure religion, which is undefiled before
God. I break all covenants with the spirit that
killed Christ—the "religious spirit"! Jesus, You
are Lord in this area of my life. Amen.*

If after praying this prayer these things continue to
operate in your life, you should seek personal deliverance from someone who is experienced in deliverance
ministry. We dealt with this spirit firsthand at Spoken
Word.

One Saturday evening, our team was called to the
church for an emergency deliverance session. Carol had
been released from a mental institution and was driven
six hours to meet with us. We were in the parking lot
when the car drove up.

What I am about to tell you may be hard to believe,
because I struggled with it even though I saw it with my
own eyes. When they pulled on the church grounds, the
entire car began to shake. A little woman about forty-
five years old stepped out of the car, talking to herself.
As I came closer to her I heard these words come out of
her mouth: "Yea, Kim can't cast me out. She never dealt
with a demon like this before. Benny Hinn can't cast me
out. You do not know who I am."

We had not seen a demon that talked this way before, and the voice coming from Carol was totally demonic. The woman was comatose, but the spirits used her body fluently. My husband and I were accompanied by two ex-witches and an ex-prostitute. We were so shocked by what we saw, we sat down and watched the demon walk around the room (through the woman's body) and quote scriptures.

We were all breathless! Carol's family had been in church for many generations, and she had been in church all of her life. The spirit revealed itself to us as a "religious spirit." We had not heard of such a thing. The demon mocked us and said, "I prophesy and quote scriptures like the Son of God. Everything you can do, I can do better!"

Many people get offended when I mention the religious spirit. But these spirits killed Christ. They are legitimate enemies of God. They are "demons of the letter," and 2 Corinthians 3:6 tells us that the letter kills. There is only one spirit that kills: satan comes to steal, kill and destroy. There is one thief, one murderer and one destroyer. He does not care if he uses a sawed-off shotgun or a brand-new Bible to do his dirty work.

We took a deep breath, shook ourselves, accepted the truth of what we were confronting and began to work those devils over like a jack hammer. Thank God for the Holy Ghost. We did not know where to start, but the prophetic anointing of God came in and gave us direction. We pleaded the blood of Jesus over that room and took authority over the boldness of the devils we were dealing with.

The demons began to beg for us to leave them

alone. We could hear them crying as they came out of the woman's body. They seemed to be far away, but the voices got closer as they exited the woman's body. God blessed us to discover the entry point of the devils in Carol's life. She owned a house no one lived in, and the demons kept saying, "Wait until we get her back into that house!"

The night she was taken to the mental institution she was caught breaking into the house through a window. She cut her body crawling through the broken glass in the window frame. Her obsession with the house was ungodly. It was located two houses from her mother's home where she grew up. As a child, she would often run away to break into this home. No one revealed this to us except the Lord. That is why prophecy is such an important tool during deliverance sessions.

Carol's mother explained to us that she was unbearable to live with and took much attention to care for. After many hours of deliverance, Carol got a major breakthrough. She is not running away, and demons are not speaking through her anymore. She has a new glow on her face, and I see her at conferences all the time. She is living a normal life because the spirit of torment has been broken off of her life.

God wants His people to be in a place to hear from Him, and religion is the greatest hindrance. If you believe I have a personal problem with religion, then this teaching is already helping you. You are discerning accurately! I hate religion because God hates it. It is one of the worst subliminal bondages in the body of Christ.

When our discerners are sharpened to hear God's voice, we will not listen to or follow the strange voices of the enemy.

> But he that entereth in by the door is the shepherd of the sheep.
>
> — JOHN 10:2

Let us review how to recognize the counterfeit.

> Now there are diversities of gifts, but the same spirit. And there are differences of administrations but the same Lord. And there are diversities of operations but it is the same God which worketh all in all...To another faith by the same spirit: to another the gifts of healing by the same spirit; to another the working of miracles; to another prophecy; to another discerning of spirits; to another diverse kinds of tongues; to another interpretation of tongues...If the foot shall say, Because I am not the hand, I am not of the body; it is therefore not of the body? And if the ear shall say, Because I am not the eye, I am not of the body; is it therefore not of the body? If the whole body were an eye, where were the hearing? If the whole were hearing, where were the smelling? But now hath God set the same members every one of them in body, as it has pleased him.
>
> — 1 CORINTHIANS 12:4–6, 9–10, 15–19

Based on this passage, I would like to make several points.

1. There are many different kinds of gifts.

2. Under the category of these gifts are many

different functions or ways they operate.

3. All of these gifts operate by the same spirit.

4. All of these gifts are submitted to one God, who is Jesus Christ.

God designed the body, and He knew what He was doing. I believe this is why He made the apostolic and prophetic five-fold ministry gifts the foundation of the household of faith.

…And are built upon the foundation of the apostles and prophets, Jesus Christ himself being the chief corner stone.

—EPHESIANS 2:20

For every gift that God has given, the enemy has sent a counterfeit.

It will take an apostolic mantle and prophetic intervention to set order in the house when it comes to the diversity of the gifting of God. It is urgent to note that when Jeremiah set order, he started by rooting out and digging up some stuff. (See Jeremiah 1.) For every gift that God has given, the enemy has sent a counterfeit. James said every good and perfect gift is from above and cometh down from the Father of lights, with whom there is no variableness, neither shadow of turning.

The soothsayer followed the apostles for days without any notice. She was not chanting or throwing voodoo dust. She was quoting scriptures. The Bible says the devil comes as an angel of light. I believe that this encounter in the Book of Acts was prophetic in many ways. Many people who are operating in "other" spirits have followed the church quoting scriptures for too long. This is the season when the apostolic mantle of God is going to fall on the church and publicly reveal the counterfeits.

We have had much infiltration from the other side in our local church. There are so many aspects of this issue that I cannot discuss now because people are just not ready for it. And when I say "people," I mean most saved people. The folk on the dark side know just what I'm talking about. Every time we open the church doors the enemy comes in. He comes to steal, kill and destroy! If you are doing something for the Lord that is giving life, you can bet the enemy will be there to destroy it. I am not speaking of the devil personified by the world as the little cartoon character. I am talking about the spirit that jumps in people and walks in the door and sits on the first row.

I have no problem sharing this because I have experienced situations that qualify me to tell about it. I have always said, "If you can pass the test, you can tell the testimony." I was spending time with a pastor and his wife after a service one night, and my conversation veered off into a topic I do not mention often—the queen of the coast. This is one of the highest levels of voodoo and occult activity that exists. Out of nowhere the words slipped out of my mouth, "Do you know about the people who operate under the water?" I asked them if they had ever heard of the term "BaBa," which is a high-level warlock priest. I never understood why I mentioned this to these pastors. They stared at me with a strange stare and went on to another conversation.

Months later these pastors called me. They seemed to be alarmed. The pastor's brother had confessed to being part of a voodoo group that operates under the water. He was trying to leave the cult, and his life was in danger. Someone had given him a drink that caused all of his organs to fail him. He accepted Jesus into his life, but the warfare was great. The pastors called me to pray for him in the hospital.

The witches had contacts on the hospital staff. When I talked to the man to pray for him, he answered in a weak voice, "Hello, this is BaBa." At the time, I had only met one Baba who confessed to being one, but the realization was too great for this ministry couple. The thing I mentioned in a casual conversation had come so close to their home. If the Holy Spirit had not spoken through me that day, they would have thought their brother needed psychiatric treatment.

God said He would not have us to be ignorant of the devices of the enemy. These spirits do not come as vampires or werewolves. They hide behind titles like "Evangelist" "Mother" "Father" and "Pastor." They are wolves in sheep clothing. Their gifts seem so similar, but we can always know them by the spirit they come in.

First Corinthians tells us the gifts of God operate by one Spirit who submits only to Him. This is how we can easily detect the counterfeit: (1) They operate by another spirit; and (2) They submit their gifts to many gods.

These spirits are so subtle. They do not come as vampires and werewolves; they come like Jesus or as another Holy Ghost. Paul had to specify and make sure the people knew which Jesus he was preaching about. He said, "And this Jesus, whom I preach unto you, is Christ" (Acts 17:3). Second Corinthians 11:4 gives a similar warning: "If he that cometh preach another Jesus whom we have not preached, or if ye receive another spirit, or another gospel, which ye have not accepted, ye might bear well with him."

Discerning of spirits is needed more than ever in the body of Christ.

These verses refer to the simplicity of the gospel. Paul was telling the church at Corinth that he feared the possibility of deception creeping into the church. He used the example of the serpent beguiling Eve through its subtlety. He told them to be watchful so their minds would not be corrupted. Discerning of spirits is needed more than ever in the body of Christ. I believe that from the reading the previous passages, we can safely say there is a counterfeit Jesus and Holy Ghost spirits, and another gospel that can be proclaimed.

This is a time in God when we must allow Him to sharpen our spiritual discerners. The Bible says if it were possible even the very elect would be deceived. There are two questions we need to answer here: (1) Who are the elect? And (2) what makes it possible for them to be deceived?

First of all, the elect are those separated and chosen by God. They can only be led astray if they pretend the enemy is not there. The elect know their God! The real key is that every good soldier must also have an awareness of his enemy. If we pretend that there is only one gospel, one Jesus and one Holy Ghost, we deceive ourselves. This is the curse of the "beautiful gospel." God never promised us a beautiful gospel, He covenanted with us to give us the truth—which is the only thing that makes men free.

Chapter V

IDOLATRY

Christians are not the only ones who can discern spirits. Psychics operate through a demonic counterfeit of this gift that is legitimately real in the spirit. I believe some of these people have the high calling of God on their lives, but they are serving the creature rather than the Creator. Because everything in life falls into two categories—creature or Creator—the devil has no choice but to be a creature. God Almighty is the Creator—all by Himself. The devil hates the fact that he is not the creator because he always wants to be on top.

Psychics operate in a counterfeit power governed

by the creature, satan, and derived from other gods and another spirit. An example of a psychic god is the Khari shell. While these fetishes have become fads, with people wearing them in their hair, around their ankles, as necklaces and even on their clothing, they are used to worship voodoo gods and harness more divination power. These objects are worshiped, and they have been dedicated to demons.

Object worship is very popular, and every culture has a form of it. I have spent a lot of time in Hong Kong in the last few years, and the idolatry and object worship there is very obvious. But we have our cultural gods in America as well. *For every Buddha in a shopping window in China, we have Rolex watches and Rolls Royce cars in our American showcases.* The key thing to remember about object worship is that the actual object has no power, but there is a demon assigned to the object. The demon behind the Buddha is witchcraft and temple worship. The demon behind the American objects of worship I mentioned is the spirit of mammon.

The essence of idolatry is that the affection of that spirit is attached to or released on the person or place. There is nothing wrong with having nice, expensive things, but God hates it when these objects take His place in our hearts. The Greek word for *mammon* is *mammona*, and it means "money personified." We have to be careful not to form a relationship or soul tie with money. This is why God hates idols; they take up the space He wants to occupy. God wants to become real in our lives, yet money will take on a reality in our lives that is deadly.

In the world, people will sometimes say, "You look like money." This is because money can personify itself in our lives. When people see us they should not see money; they should see Jesus! The awesomeness of this is that when they see Jesus, they will not see a poverty spirit. This is not because I look to Jesus to give me prosperity; I seek all of Him. But because Jesus *is* prosperity, when I receive the fullness of Him, I receive all that He is.

While writing this chapter, God revealed to me we take on the characteristics of anything that occupies space in our hearts. Just like the natural heart pumps blood to the other parts of the body; so does the spiritual heart release idolatry throughout our being. The Bible warns us to give no place, or room, to the devil.

Neither give place to the devil.

—EPHESIANS 4:27

Jesus wants to take up all the space in our hearts; He does not want to share it with any person, place or thing.

All of mankind was created in the image of God, but when Adam fell, the sinful nature of man was birthed into the earth realm. This sinful nature represents the essence of what the devil is made of. The Bible says iniquity—including perversion, mischief and sin—was found in Lucifer. (See Isaiah 14.) Ezekiel 14:3 goes on to say that men have set up their idols in their hearts and put the stumbling block of their iniquity before their face. After the demonic transaction took place in the spirit in the Garden of Eden, man took on the characteristics of satan. When Eve allowed the

73

thoughts of the devil to enter her mind, she took on the nature of what occupied a space in her mind. Eve then transferred the same spirit to Adam.

Sin is ugly, and if we partake of it, we will begin to look like it.

This brings me to the subject of the new birth. This marks the beginning of the process of man's restoration to the image of God. Sin is ugly, and if we partake of it, we will begin to look like it. We resemble Jesus when we allow Him to take His rightful place in our hearts. It is all about having the order of God in our lives. Order always operates in the light because anything done in obscurity will bring disorder and confusion. The Bible says we must be careful that the light in us be not darkness. (See Luke 11:35.) The truth of this message is highlighted in verse 33 of that same passage: "No man, when he hath lighted a candle, putteth it in a secret place, neither under a bushel, but on a candlestick, *that they that come in may see the light*" (emphasis added).

Revival has been the cry of the church since it began. I believe that until the people who have accepted Jesus Christ as Savior have been revived, we cannot revive the people we are trying to win. Jesus wants to be more than our Savior; He wants to reign as Lord in our hearts. But He cannot reign as Lord in someone's life until that person sees the light. To be saved means we have come out of the kingdom of darkness, but to receive the lordship of Jesus Christ we must go into the marvelous light.

Luke 11:33 says "that they that have come in must see the light." One of the greatest evangelistic tools we can ever use is "spiritual maintenance." We are trying to win a lost and dying world, but "the ones that have come in" are dying on the pews. The devil does not care if you die spiritually in the world or in the church. The new converts must see the light. They must come into the house of God and see the difference. If we are worshiping the same gods in the church as people in the world, the new converts will walk in obscurity. They must see the light! Idolatry breeds obscurity, and where there is obscurity, the people will have no certainty and backslide.

The main assignment of idolatry is to hide the light of Christ in our lives. One of the Greek words for idolatry is *eidololatreia.* This word refers to "image worship," or worshiping things that can be seen. When Moses did not move fast enough for the children of Israel, they fashioned their own god. They asked Aaron to "make gods that would go before them," or gods they could see. (See Exodus 32.) They could only follow God when they saw Moses. This brings up a very important point. Moses had become a type of idol to the people because when he was not present they began to serve other gods. It is important that leaders provide the people a foundation that would challenge them to keep their eyes on Jesus.

This is what a true apostolic foundation does; it builds ministry that can continue to flow even in the absence of the leader. Aaron fashioned a molten calf and said, "These be thy gods which brought thee up out of the land of Egypt." Notice that it was one calf but many gods. For every physical idol, there are many demons behind it. It is also interesting to note that Jeroboam made two calves of gold for the people in 1 Kings 12:28. He presented them to the people and said, "Behold thy gods, O Israel, which brought thee up and out of the land of Egypt." In both cases, the people saw these gods as a type of deliverance.

Throughout history the people of God have depended on idols to "bring them out." They wanted something tangible to represent a higher power in their lives. Even secular drug treatment programs promote "higher powers" because they believe people need something bigger than themselves to see them through. I do not believe in programs like Alcoholic and Narcotics Anonymous because they promote idolatry. A support group is a good thing, but Christians must be careful of what the group is supporting. Many of these programs teach things that contradict the word of God. Addiction is a "devil problem." To overcome it, people need a "Jesus answer"!

Besides all of this, these programs simply do not work. They are only temporal and always leave the person thinking, "I am a recovering addict, and I will have this weakness for the rest of my life." They create what I call the "spirit of the seeker." These people are always looking and never finding. In 2 Timothy, the Bible says they are forever learning but never able to come to the true knowledge.

> Ever learning, and never able to come to the knowl-
> edge of the truth.
>
> —2 TIMOTHY 3:7

I am so glad I am not a *recovering* drug addict; I have *recovered* because whom the Son makes free is free indeed. That means that there are no ifs, ands or buts about it. I am free because the truth has made me free.

There is a big difference in feeling better and being free indeed.

People cannot be set free unless we tell them the truth. The truth is that Sister Sally is not addicted to cocaine because she has a personality complex. Sister Sally has a spirit of addiction. We can feed her emotions and make her feel better for the rest of her life, or we can lead her to a place where Jesus will "make her free." There is a big difference in feeling better and being free indeed. Feelings will eventually run out, but even when I do not feel good I am still delivered. Besides, getting deliverance from an addiction does not always feel good. There is a disciplining aspect of deliverance from any addiction, and discipline definitely does not feel good!

Paul said that he had to buffet his body. Even after God makes us free, it is submission to His instructions that keeps us free indeed. Secular organizations that attempt to take the place of the delivering power of God are modern-day manifestations of the golden calves. Today people are saying the same thing as the children of Israel: "These are the gods that have delivered us!"

People often want gods they can visualize, and today we have many gods we can see on a daily basis. I am amazed at the deception the enemy has released to make Christian women proud to call themselves divas. I have come across several cases where born-again women casually used this name to reference themselves. A *diva* is defined as "a female goddess that is worshiped." While doing a word search on the word *diva*, I was referred to an entry for "Shiva," a Hindu goddess known as the lord of the dance. On an evangelistic trip in Malaysia, I came across an article written about Oprah Winfrey that addressed her as a television goddess. Famous artists and singers such as Whitney Houston, Mariah Carey and Britney Spears proudly call themselves divas.

The Bible tells us the three-fold cord of the world is the lust of the flesh, the lust of the eyes and the pride of life. How many people desire to be like these famous images that God set before our eyes. There was once a commercial that jokingly said everybody wants to be like Mike (Michael Jordan). The truth is that people really do want to be like Mike and all he represents: money (the lust of the flesh), fame (the pride of life) and success (the lust of the eyes).

Though these are not statues or temples, they are all images. Behind each one of them there is misery and despair without Jesus Christ. People who experience these false glories in their lives are number one candidates for suicide, depression, addiction and much more. I have several friends who have very prestigious positions in life, and it is not what it appears to be from the outside. It is only an image. My friend Karla grew up with me. She would dance and sing in front of the mirror all of the time. Even when she was a little girl,

Karla knew she was going to be a star when she grew up. She wanted to sing and be famous. She was fat, and I do not remember her having a nice voice, but today Karla sings on one of the biggest record labels in the hip-hop industry. She travels among the rich and the famous all the time, and she is not fat anymore; she looks like Janet Jackson and can hit notes that will shatter glass.

We minister to Karla all the time. She has a fear for the things of God on the inside of her, but because of her environment it is hard for her to sell out to Jesus. She battles with depression all the time, yet everyone around her comes to her for prayer. She told me that behind the scenes, everyone is depressed and troubled. This is one of the reasons addiction is strong in the music industry. People are barely making it. They have all that they ever dreamed of in the natural, but there is still something missing in their lives.

I can relate to that feeling. I remember wanting to be the fastest female sprinter in the nation when I was in junior college. Not only did I become the fastest woman in the nation at the time, but I also held two national records. I later became the fastest woman in the armed forces (Army, Marines, Navy and Air Force) and held the spot for three years. This may not seem like a lot to you, but it was the manifestation of my greatest dream. Can you imagine? What if the thing that you have wanted all of your life walks through your front door? Would you be set in life? The truth is, if you made a wish list of ten things and they all came to pass in the morning, without Jesus you would still be miserable!

When I won some of the biggest awards in track and field, outside the Olympics, I left the ceremony and went to my room and cried. God made us to worship Him. No matter how successful we are in life, we will feel empty without Jesus Christ. He put a vacuum on the inside of us that is always drawing and pulling, and we must be careful of what we allow our hearts to pull on. The goal of idolatry is to block the suction in our lives that should be drawing from the Most High God. It is amazing to me how easy it is to be idolatrous in everyday life issues. The Hebrew word for *idol*, *eidolotatreia*, also means "to produce something in likeness or resemblance." It means to reproduce or represent the essence of a thing. The significance of an idol is not how it manifests itself in the physical, but what it actually represents in the spirit. To understand the essence of idolatry, we must take a look at the term *fetish*.

A fetish is an inanimate object (natural or cultural) believed to have magical powers. It is a tool of witchcraft that has a demon assigned to it. A fetish with great power is often considered *taboo*, a Polynesian word that refers to a sacred, consecrated or unclean object (Merriam-Webster's Collegiate Dictionary). Though the actual word *fetish* is not in Scripture, the Bible has a lot to say about the subject. God gave the people specific instructions about the groves and asherah poles, which depicts the male phallus or private part in reverence to the fertility gods. These poles are identical to the Washington Monument, and there are many located in all major cities. They have the same symbolic value as the pyramid and the "all-seeing eye" on the dollar bill. These symbols are examples of emblems that have more meaning than the natural eye can see. They are all fetishes of Egypt and have Masonic roots. God said:

> Do not look to the altars or the work of their hands. Have no respect for that which the fingers have made.
>
> —Isaiah 17:8

In this same scripture, God referred to *graven* images. In Exodus 20:3–4 God said He did not want any other God placed before Him and that we were not to make unto ourselves any graven image. The word *graven* means "to be carved with the hand." Earlier we mentioned Joshua and how he and his generation acquired a new attitude that gave them entrance into the land of milk and honey. We must realize that in the land of milk and honey there were not only giants, but also other gods. Joshua 7 gives an indepth description of what went on at the Battle of Ai.

The people of Ai were small in number and had heard about the strength of Joshua's army. Ai was in no way a threat, and upon the advice of his elders, Joshua sent only three thousand men. But the small tribe of Ai defeated these three thousand warriors. Devastated, Joshua rent his clothes, and he and his elders put dust on their heads. The word *dust* in this story is *aphar,* and means that they were "made shame and brought to nothing." Joshua cried out to God in despair, and God's response was: "Get up. Why are you laying on your face praying? Israel has sinned!" There is no sense in fasting, praying and crying out to God if we have not dealt with the sin in our lives. God said His people had done the following:

↦ Sinned against God

↦ Transgressed their covenant with God

↦ Took of the accursed thing

↦ Partake of the accursed thing and put it amongst their own stuff

Obedience is better than sacrifice.

Knowing the story of Joshua, one naturally wonders what went wrong. God had promised him that *no man* would stand before him. God told Joshua that everywhere the sole of his foot tread according to the coast he had given him was subject to him. God kept His word. No man stood before Joshua that day; a demon of disobedience did. The Scripture reminds us that obedience is better than sacrifice.

> And Samuel said, Hath the Lord as great delight in burnt offerings and sacrifices, as in obeying the voice of the Lord? Behold, to obey is better than sacrifice, and to hearken than the fat of rams.
> —1 SAMUEL 15:22

King Saul was removed for the same reason: idolatry! God told Saul to utterly destroy Amalek and all they had because God did not want His people to partake of the contamination of the idols of the

Amalekites. God knew they had dedicated their objects to devils. All of their belongings had curses attached to them. This is what the phrase "accursed thing" means—that which has been dedicated unto devils. When Joshua defeated Jericho and the walls came down, he warned the people:

> Shout for the Lord has given you the city. And the city shall be accursed, even it, and all that are in it, to the Lord. Only Rahab and her house shall live because she hid the messengers that we sent. And you, in any wise keep yourself from the accursed thing, lest you make yourself accursed, when you take of the accursed thing and make the camp of Israel a curse, and trouble it.

There are two Hebrew words for *accursed* that I would like to bring your attention: (1) *charam*, and (2) *cherem*. Both of these words mean "to consecrate unto evil or to be devoted as a doomed object." They also mean, "that which is cursed to the root and should be utterly destroyed!" In the case of Rahab, God's mercy was extended toward her and her household. The key word is *covenant*. Rahab broke her covenant with devils and obtained a covenant with the Most High God. Hebrews 11:31 says that by faith Rahab perished not with those who believed not. She believed and obtained favor with God that put her in the hall of faith. Now that's covenant!

Saul won the battle and lost favor with God. Joshua lost the battle but was restored after the fall. Saul spared the wicked king Agag, and Achan hid the accursed thing in his tent. Both acts represent the forming of soul ties.

Soul ties make people disobey God; they represent attachments to people and things God has commanded us to let go. After studying fetishes for some time, I have found that people can form unusual affections to items. There is a spirit of obsession that usually connects itself with this affection. I have witnessed people who have hundreds of items of the same kind and hide their obsession behind the excuse of being a collector. It is not the actual item they are attached to, but the familiar spirit assigned to the object to keep the person subliminally bound.

Many things presented to us today as fads are fetishes.

Many things presented to us today as fads are fetishes. What we see as a new style is actually a resurrection of ancient spirits. Body piercing and tattooing are both ancient pagan rituals. In Leviticus 19:28 God told the people not to make cuttings in their flesh for the dead. He also told them not to print any marks upon their flesh. When the prophets of Baal wanted to get the attention of their gods, they cut their flesh. Devils are aroused by the release of blood. Ancient occult rituals were often practiced whereby the worshiper would cut his body in a blood sacrifice to summon dead spirits. They were actually conjuring demonic power from the underworld.

It is the job of the Kosmokrator, who is the god of the world, or the ruling spirits of darkness, to blind the minds of the people.

84

In whom the god of this world hath blinded the minds of them which believe not, lest the light of the glorious gospel of Christ, who is the image of God, should shine unto them.

— 2 CORINTHIANS 4:4

For we wrestle not against flesh and blood, but against principalities, against powers, against the rulers of the darkness of this world, against spiritual wickedness in high places.

—EPHESIANS 6:12

Many people will not submit to making conscious sacrifices to devils, so the enemy deceives them through acts such as body piercing and tattooing. Parents, I pray you will discuss these matters with your children. Every time blood is released in a tattoo parlor or when someone submits himself to body piercing, it is a sacrifice unto satan. These things have become common in society, but Leviticus 10 says it is the responsibility of the priest to teach the people the difference between what is common and what is holy. Tatoos and body piercing were at one time limited to prisoners and motorcycle gangs. As evil is becoming more commonplace in our society, doctors, lawyers and even schoolteachers participate in this fad.

It is the responsibility of the priest to teach the people the difference between what is common and what is holy.

I know many will argue that I am going too far. It may seem hard to believe that an object can have that big of an effect on a person. But I have a good biblical example of how much objects can impact someone.

Bible scholars often refer to Joseph as a type of Christ. They teach messages such as, "From the Pit to the Palace" or "Poor little Joseph was the one everybody picked on." Rarely do you hear someone preach about why Joseph requested that his bones not be left in Egypt. (See Genesis 50:25.) Joseph knew the people of Egypt were hooked on fetishes. Even as I am writing this chapter on idolatry, God has blessed me to travel to Asia to study hard-core idolatry.

The people here are very superstitious and superficial—a dangerous combination. Being superstitious makes a person rely on the supernatural while the superficial part of him makes him lean on things that can be seen. In Acts 17, Paul told the people of Athens, "I perceive that you are most religious and very reverent to demons." The Athenians were well-educated, and the three-fold cord of religion, witchcraft and intellect had them in a bad place spiritually.

Paul said they were praying to "the altar of the unknown god." The word *unknown* in the Greek is pronounced *ag-noce-tos*, which is related to the English word *agnostic*. Agnostic means to be noncommittal, or not sold out to anything. The agnostic is one who has no proof of God but does not deny that He exists. An agnostic person is the greatest example of lukewarm I have seen. There are many agnostics who say that they believe in God but do not believe in going to church. I believe we can be safe to say an agnostic person is one who believes in part. If this is the case, we have many agnostics who claim to be Christians. There are Christians who say they believe in God but not in witchcraft, even though witchcraft has a very significant role in the Bible. Scripture reveals the good and the bad, which takes me back to the story of Joseph and how objects changed his walk with God.

Let us take a look at Joseph's life after he came from the pit to the palace. When he was first asked to interpret Pharoah's dream, he responded, "It is not in me to interpret the dream, but my God shall give Pharoah an answer of peace." (See Genesis 41:16.) But years later when Joseph recovers the cup from his youngest brother, his attitude totally changed. Then he said: "What have you done; do you not realize that a man such as I can certainly detect through divination?" (Genesis 44:15).

What brought Joseph to this place of idolatry? The Bible gives three clues in Genesis 41:42: Pharaoh gave Joseph his ring, which represented marriage or relationship; arrayed him in fine linen, which represented a mantle or anointing; and put a gold chain around his neck, which represented a yoke or bondage.

Idolatry is not limited to culture or time.

When many of us think of idolatry, we picture ancient biblical times, or African or Egyptian paganism. That is a trick of the enemy because idolatry is not limited to culture or time. I believe we are living in the most idolatrous era since the beginning of time. In Luke 11:29, the Bible speaks of how a wicked and adulterous generation seeks after a sign. This word *sign* in the Greek is *semeion* and means "supernatural." We are living in a day when people are seeking the supernatural at any cost. They want answers, but they are not willing to wait on God to get them.

In this passage in Luke, Jesus was saying that it is idolatry to seek supernatural power without first seeking a relationship with God. When we remove our relationship with God from the power of God, it breeds the spirit of witchcraft. This is what happened with Joseph. Witchcraft is a work of the flesh and can easily be related to power with no relationship. Relationship is how we worship, or connect, with God, and this can be done only in spirit and in truth. When the flesh gets involved it only stirs rebellion, which is as the sin of witchcraft. This is how "charismatic witchcraft" spreads throughout the church.

A simple definition for "charismatic witchcraft" is when the anointing has lifted and gifts continue to operate. The Bible says "the gifts and calling of God are without repentance" (Romans 11:29). The word *gift* noted in this passage is *charisma* in the Greek and means "divine spiritual endowment." Based on these definitions we can be safe to say the anointing—which is the seal of God's presence on a person, place or thing—can leave a person, and the divine spiritual endowments can continue to operate. God will not take these endowments back; they are without repentance! This is why it is very important that we do not seek after signs.

A sign represents what is physically visible; it represents or promotes something. Ezekiel had a vision in which he saw a wheel in the middle of the wheel. (See Ezekiel 1.) This is very significant. Ezekiel did not just stop at what he saw on the outside. He did not get caught up in the form of the thing or what it appeared to be. He had a spiritual eye to see "the essence" of the thing. In other words, the wheel in the middle of the wheel represented what made the whole thing work. Ezekiel was not interested in the body of the car; he wanted to know what kind of motor was running it. God spoke to me so clearly about Ezekiel's vision. He said, "It is the motor that determines your motive!"

We are living in a day when we cannot get too caught up in the outcome; we must consider the root. Jesus was the wheel in the middle of the wheel. I am not moved by how fast the vehicle will travel if Jesus is not the one driving. If Jesus is not steering, then the motive will always be wrong. When we look for a sign, we will get snared by the grips of idolatry. Yet when we seek relationship, we become believers.

The Bible says there are signs that will follow true believers. When we are spiritually in place, the signs will follow us, and we will not have to run after them. I believe our goal should be to have clean hands and a pure heart, not to walk in signs and wonders. When our hands are clean and our hearts are right, the signs and wonders will follow! It is the generation that seeks Him that will do the greater works. Psalm 24:3–6 describes it perfectly:

> Who shall ascend unto the hill of the Lord? Or who shall stand in His holy place? He that hath *clean*

hands and a pure heart; who hath not lifted up his soul unto vanity; nor sworn deceitfully. He shall receive the blessings from the Lord, and righteousness from the God of our salvation. This is the generation of them that seek Him; that seek Thy face, O Jacob. *Selah*.

—EMPHASIS ADDED

I hunger and thirst for the greater works, but more than that it is my desire to know Him. To know Him in the power of His resurrection, I must be willing to know Him in the fellowship of His sufferings. Idols come into our lives to do two main things:

-⊱ To bring defeat into our lives

-⊱ To separate us from the presence of God

An idol can be defined as any thing that is forbidden by God to be in our lives, or something that takes up a place in our hearts that God is supposed to occupy. It is common for people to see things that come before God as idols, but things that should not be in our lives at all are idols, too. The devil will trick us into believing we can keep certain things in our lives as long as we keep them at bay. Achan kept the accursed thing in his possession. It was dedicated to the demonic and forbidden by God. Anything that God forbids becomes an idol if we partake of it.

The subject of idolatry brings so many things to my natural mind, but understanding the true depths of all that is behind idolatry is something I can discern only spiritually. When I think of the generation that will seek the face of God, the first person who comes to my mind

90

is a young woman that we ministered to in Malaysia named Eliza. I know that there are some things that I am about to share that may seem hard to swallow. You may want to review the teaching that I have done earlier on "the natural man" before you read this story. What I am about to tell you is true. I have changed the names to protect the individuals involved.

You have to make up your mind about me right now. Either I am a crazy preacher who is writing a bunch of foolishness, or I am a woman of God who has experienced some real things in the spirit realm and is not afraid to tell about it. I call this story "My Modern-Day Mount Carmel Experience." If you're still with me, read on.

Chapter VI

MY MODERN-DAY MOUNT CARMEL EXPERIENCE

My husband and I and a team of three arrived in Sitiawan, Malaysia, to rest for a day before we began a crusade. We had just ministered for a week in Hong Kong, and after much travel, we were in need of some recreational time. We stopped to visit the building where the crusade would be held and to meet our escort, who was to take us shopping. The pastor wanted us to see the inside of the facility, but as I walked into the door, I was inquiring about the market for shopping in the city.

Then without any warning, the Spirit of God came into the room and began to speak to me. It would have seemed rude in the natural, as I quickly cut the conversation off with the pastor and began to walk around the room listening to God. Everyone in the room automatically began to worship the Lord. We did not even dare look at each other as the Holy Spirit commanded our attention. I began to write the word of the Lord as God spoke to me.

He told me I was standing on Mount Carmel and that I was to put the princes of the land to open shame. He told me to release His handmaidens and to break the dedications of the grounds. As God spoke these words to me, I failed to fully understand what He was saying. Little did I know my experience with Eliza would shed light and revelation to every word that proceeded from God's mouth to me.

Eliza was in her early thirties and had attractive features. But on this day, the grim darkness around her was not a pretty scene. I was told I had a special ministry case that required private attention, but I had no idea how serious it was. My husband briefed me about this young woman, telling me she had endured much ritualistic abuse. Though we have dealt with many cases of ritualistic abuse, I was about to embark on a realm I had never experienced before. The young woman had strange manifestations during the service, and my husband and the team gave her personal ministry during the day sessions.

On the first night, I was alarmed to find out that a bat had flown over my head during the entire service. I thanked God He never let me see the creature because I felt as if I was not ready for this kind of encounter. By the way, that was the name of the crusade: "Encounter 2002." Having a bat flying over my head while I was preaching was an encounter I felt I could actually do without.

The most ironic thing was that the room was lit up with camera lights and the works. I was under the impression that bats could not endure light; they are creatures of the night. While my husband was ministering to Eliza, she told him the bat was sent by the evil ones to torment her because she had given her life to Jesus. She said as the bat flew across the room, he was releasing pains to her head.

On the second night, I took a leap of faith when the bat appeared over the stage as they called my name to start preaching. I am not a pet lover, and bats are surely not my cup of tea. Large bugs give me the creeps, so I had to have a resolve in my spirit to walk upon that stage with my bat "friend" waiting on me. As I began to pray, the bat disappeared into the curtains and never showed up again that night.

I approached the pastor after this service and asked him if the ministry had problems with bats on a regular basis. He gently smiled at me and told me that the bats came when Eliza joined the church. My natural mind was running overtime. I tried not to overreact. Everyone seemed so calm about the situation, and I did not want to be the one to lose it. My team sat on the front row with their eyes big and their mouths wide open as a bat swooped over their apostle's head. Being the demon-busters, it would seem we would know what to do in a situation like this!

To tell you the truth, not only did we not know what to do, we did not even know how to act. Finally, the pastor took me off to the side and explained Eliza's history. The story he told me about her did not make matters any better; now I knew what the Lord meant when He welcomed me to Mount Carmel.

Eliza fell in love with a man at a party many years ago. He took her to a hotel the first night they met, and they continued to see each other for a while. Eliza was a virgin when she met him. She was very young and had hopes that this would be her husband. Later in the relationship she found out that he was married and had no plans to marry her. He cut off the relationship and left Eliza in despair. Not willing to give up that easily, Eliza flew to Thailand and made an appointment with the highest level warlock in the land, who just happens to be the wealthiest, most famous temple monk in the world.

Eliza went to Thailand to obtain power to put a curse on this man to make him leave his wife and marry her. She spent four days and three nights with some of the highest level warlocks in the known world. The monks and the demons had sex with her every night. First, I think it is important to explain how a demon can have sex with a person. This occurred in the Scriptures.

In Genesis 6 the Bible talks about how the sons of God came down and had sex with the daughters of men. Today, I know these spirits as Incubus and Succubus. *Webster's Dictionary* refers to both of these spirits as demon entities that attack men and women sexually in their sleep. The demons may present themselves in a dream as someone the person knows or as a person who is secretly admired. I have done personal ministry to several prostitutes, and they have constant encounters with these spirits. Too many of them have described the worst form of these demons in the same way. These spirits actually look like monsters, but they disguise themselves to resemble what the person desires.

If a man looks at a woman to lust after her, he has already committed adultery.

In counseling sessions with saved women, I discovered that many have entertained these spirits and used this type of activity as a means of abstaining from fornication. They were having sexual affairs in their dream lives. The Bible says that if a man looks at a woman to lust after her, he has already committed adultery. It is the same with entertaining sex demons. This is why masturbation is a sin; it is a sin of the imagination. God destroyed the entire world by flood because of the imaginations of men. (See Genesis 6.) Lucifer was cast out of heaven because of what he imagined to do.

Sex is never a solo act. The masturbator may think he or she is alone, but a door is opened to sexual union with nightmare spirits. The act that starts out as a fantasy of enjoyment will eventually end up as a demonic nightmare of torment. The Scripture tells us that when sin finishes its course, it opens the door to death.

The goal of the enemy is to impregnate its victim with a Cambion—the seed of satan that is planted into an individual as a result of intercourse with these nightmare spirits. Incubus and Succubus spirits drop Cambions into the spiritual womb of the person. This is why Paul said, "In Christ Jesus I have begotten you through the gospel" (1 Corinthians 4:15). Every man and woman has a spiritual womb. We were all made to produce and multiply. The devil wants us to become manufacturers of his wickedness, but we were born to give birth to God's glory.

The Scriptures warn us that God hates seven things. One of them is "a heart that deviseth wicked imaginations" (Proverbs 6:18). One encounter with sexual demons does not necessarily mean that a demonic pregnancy has taken place, just as intercourse in the natural does not always lead to pregnancy. But every time intercourse takes place there is a chance that a pregnancy will occur.

Continual encounters with these spirits can result in a Cambion pregnancy, which are quite popular in Africa. They are often referred to as fathom pregnancies. Sometimes the stomach of the women will actually grow as if they were really having a baby. Women have been known to endure pregnancies of this sort for up to two years. I have personally cast demons out of people with these spirits. I have also encountered many conflicts with witches that have willingly taken on the seed of satan to have more power and rank in the dark kingdom.

Many women have ignorantly entertained these spirits out of desperation when they were barren.

Throughout the Bible God has delivered many women from the spirit of barrenness. When barrenness is the problem, the solution is to believe God and wait on Him. Impatience in this area can open a door to a false spirit. Women who are not really pregnant can begin to experience all the symptoms of a natural pregnancy through these deceiving spirits.

Another way these spirits enter a person is through the spirits of lust. It should not be acceptable for people to have constant dreams of sexual encounters or to experience uncontrollable orgasms during their sleep. When I was growing up, I would hear people refer to this as a wet dream. This was considered acceptable and normal. Today, I know this is demonic. These acts should not be tolerated in the life of a Christian. We have ministered to many people who are under these kinds of attacks; some are at a point where the demons attack them while they are consciously awake.

We should especially sit down and talk with our children about this subject. All doors to attack their sexuality must be closed. A lack of knowledge in this area could be detrimental. When a person is attacked in this manner they should bind the nightmare spirits and call them by name (Incubus, Succubus, Cambion). These spirits have no rights to operate in the life of a believer. I have never ministered to a person who wanted to be set free from this type of bondage who was not immediately delivered. If you or someone you know are being tormented by these spirits, the steps to deliverance are simple:

1. Repent of entertaining these spirits (either

knowingly or unknowingly).

2. Renounce any sexual acts or acquaintances that may have opened the door to the spirits.

3. Take authority over these spirits by binding them in Jesus' name (call them out by name).

4. Plead the blood of Jesus over you and your family (these spirits are contagious).

5. Thank God for the victory over these unclean spirits.

Now, let us get back to Eliza. Some of the stories Eliza told us about her four-day encounter in the temple in Thailand are too gross to share. However, I can tell you she had a marriage ceremony to the prince of darkness himself, satan. She vowed to never be married to a physical man, and she was to give birth to the seed of satan. This was a type of covenant-breaking spirit assigned to her whereby she would never be able to have a successful relationship with a man. Many demons will try to marry themselves to people so they cannot have a successful marriage. Demonic marriage can occur as the result of orgies, homosexuality, ritualistic sex acts through witchcraft, adultery, fornication, pornography and much more.

These are just a few things that can open these doors. The person is eventually bound to the spirit because they have broken covenant with God and have come into agreement with the spirit. We often have heard demons declare that the person being delivered was their wife or husband during deliverance manifestations. The spirits spoke through the person's mouth declaring that they had a right to be there.

Thirty months ago Eliza met Rev. Kay Chung and gave her life to the Lord. For thirty months this pastor and his congregation have ministered to this young woman to set her free from the grips of satan. When she first gave her life to Jesus, the demons visited her every night to rape her. God delivered her from the demonic violations of her body at an early stage. But the bondage she was still in was more than she could bear. There were black and blue marks covering her entire body. When I first met her, Eliza could not look into my eyes. When I asked her to look into my eyes, she responded by growling at me.

My heart went out to her as the reverend and his wife told me that more than three thousand needles and nails came out of her body when they ministered deliverance to her. I know this may be hard to believe, but I personally witnessed pins coming out of the top of her head when we called the devils out of her. Everyone in the village church was afraid of her because of the strong demonic manifestations she would exhibit in the services. It was not until after a few days of the meetings that I realized that there was a connection between Eliza and the bat.

During a private session in the pastor's office, four bats and an owl appeared from nowhere and began to attack Eliza's head. The pastor killed the creatures in his office. These were all creatures of the night, and they appeared in a room that had *no* windows or place of entrance. Again, I know that this story may be hard to believe, but American churches are so sheltered. Our attitude about the devil is so subliminal. He is just a cartoon character with a pitchfork and a pointed tail. We redefine demonic attacks in our society. Demonic possession is being couched in medical terms and is psychologically evaluated. We either lock up people's minds with medication, or we lock up their bodies in mental institutions because we do not know what else to do with them.

I am not saying that everything is the devil or that there are not some genuine cases of mental illness. What I am saying is that a lot of things that were demonic have been passed off to professionals when they should have been taken care of by the church. If revival broke out in the world and the professionals ran all of their cases to the church, would we know where to begin? Satan is the god of this world and the prince of the power of the air. But Jesus is Lord of all. Principalities are limited to the rank of prince, but there is only one King.

Principalities are limited to the rank of prince, but there is only one King.

I have heard people say that satan is lord of the airways. I disagree. He is the prince of the power of the air, but Jesus is King of all the heavens. This means that even though satan rules over the children of disobedience, as believers we are seated in heavenly places with Christ Jesus. In the spirit, this place is far above all principalities and every dominion named. Not only is Jesus king, but He has given us authority to reign in His stead in the earth realm. We have regained the dominion that Adam lost.

This takes me back to the word God gave me about the princes over Malaysia. Dealing with Eliza made me understand that there was a battle for her soul taking place in the spirit realm. This woman was dedicated to be the bride of satan. The Bible says that if the princes had known, they would not have killed the King of glory. I believe that if satan had known, he would have left this little girl alone. The principalities that chose her never thought she would fall in love with Jesus and dedicate herself to Him. During her quest for power, she made a death vow to one day commit suicide and join her husband (the devil) in hell. Now she has made a greater vow to the Lord of lords to spend eternity with Him.

With all the people of that small town looking on, there was a showdown in the spirit. Either the prophets of Thailand were serving the true god, or I was. Eliza's case had to be the fire that would set ablaze the wet wood before the people of this town. On the first night I preached on the topic "Mount Carmel." I declared that I had not come with enticing words of men but in demonstration of God's power. I made this declaration before a nation that was celebrating Muhammad's birthday as a national holiday. We were in a Muslim country where the women were wrapped up in religious garb from the top of their heads to the bottom of their feet. Every woman on the streets of Malaysia who did not have on a head cover for Allah had a dot in the middle of their forehead to the god of Hinduism.

Sacrifices to every kind of god in the form of

flowers, fruits and candles were all over the city streets. Everybody had a god to serve, but nobody was free. I was not told that it was illegal to witness to Muslims in Malaysia. In the services a young boy was brought before me for prayer. A man frantically alerted me that the boy was not a Christian. I thought his statement was crazy. I was thinking, *I know he is not a Christian. That is why we need to lead him to the Lord.*

Later I found out that the man who alerted me was the leader of a group of underground Muslims who had been converted to Jesus. He was warning me that I could go to jail for such a public act if it were reported. In tears, this man shared how his life is at stake every day. The goal of his ministry is to get the Muslims converted to Jesus Christ. The lives of his family and children are at risk on a daily basis for the gospel.

Faith that is never challenged never grows.

Most of you reading this story probably do not have to make these kinds of sacrifices for the gospel of Jesus Christ. I believe the least you can do is to be open to the truth about what persecuted Christians are going through today. It is very dangerous to be too comfortable as a Christian. We should always stay in a place to have things in our lives that challenge our faith. Faith that is never challenged never grows. I believe this story is one that will challenge your faith.

The familiar spirit is the greatest enemy of our faith.

It binds us up to believe only what we are familiar with. The Bible never tells us to believe what is familiar to us. The Scripture really says that what we see in the natural is not what is actually happening in the spirit. It declares that we should try the spirit of a thing to see if it is of God or not. If we judge things by natural familiarity we will be doomed to deception. On the other hand, if we ask God to show us the spirit that is behind what we are facing, we cannot go wrong. If God is the spirit behind a thing, we do not have to understand it with our natural mind.

The Bible says we should not lean to our own understanding but *acknowledge* the Lord in all of our ways, and He will direct our path. The word *acknowledge* is very important in this verse of scripture. It shows us that if we can acknowledge the fact that God is involved, we do not have to understand; we just need to trust Him. Trust in God always leads us to ultimate understanding. When Abraham laid Isaac on the altar, I am sure he did not understand. But he trusted God. He told the young men with him that he and the boy were going to worship God, but they would return. He did not have the details of how they would return, but he knew God would never leave or forsake him.

When Abraham obeyed God through his trust, God revealed the overall picture to him in the end. As a reader you need to make a decision right now. Is God in the contents of the story you are reading now? In the spirit there are only two authors: God and the devil. The devil is the author of confusion, and Jesus is the author and finisher of our faith. Ask yourself, "Is Kimberly Daniels a credible witness in the natural and in the spirit?" If you believe God is in this story, do not allow your natural mind to talk you out of the truth. (Satan comes to steal, kill and destroy, but Jesus came that we might have life.) Is this story about abundant life? We need to consider who is getting the glory out of this story. Just as Abraham told the young men with him, I am telling you, we are about to go somewhere you may not understand. My promise to you is that we will be back!

I promise not to take you out there and leave you hanging. The devil is defeated by the blood of the Lamb and the word of our testimony. In many cultures it is not proper to open your skeletons and let people see into your closet. Although a testimony has to be told in the timing of God, I am a witness that the further you have to go back into your closet, the more people it will bless. Some of the things I am about to share with you will take you there. Where is *there*? Probably, to most of you reading this book, some of the things I am sharing will take you to another level in the spirit realm.

The Word of the Lord declares that we cannot please God without faith. I pray that the eye of your understanding will be enlightened as you read the remainder of the story, in Jesus' name!

Though many people did not know the details of her story, Eliza was known in the community as a demon-possessed person. Our mission in Malaysia was to declare the lordship of Jesus Christ in the country.

Was Jesus Lord enough to set Eliza free? You may wonder why a person of faith, like me, asks a question like that. This is the question I could sense from the looks in the eyes of the people. Just like on Mount Carmel, the people watched to see whose god would answer by fire. Eliza's case seemed so terminal. While she received deliverance from the occult spirits, the idols physically manifested themselves and came through her womb as if she were having birth. The four-to six-inch idol statues that came from her womb were placed into jars of anointed oil. The ministry team took a break, and when they returned the idols mysteriously disappeared from the jars.

On the night before the last night of the meeting, the bat met me on the stage again. This time the creepy creature seemed bolder than before. It darted over the heads of the people with fervor. I tried to focus on what I was preaching, but the flying animal swooped down closer to me as the time passed. I began to rebuke the devil, and the bat started running into the walls of the sanctuary. It seemed as though the flying rodent was drunk. My heart was beating fast, and just as I was about to get afraid, I got mad at the devil. I thought, *How dare he interrupt the service of God?* I made up my mind that even the physical enemy I was facing would not deter me from my assignment that night.

It was me or the bat, and I decided to stand. At the end of service that night, I knew I was encountering a level of warfare. I was a little disappointed the bat did not drop dead when I rebuked it. I even prayed that it would come out after the service because I knew it was not illegal to kill a bat. I felt like the team and I could get a club and end the nightmare when everyone left the church. I was mad at the devil, and I truly wanted to physically take it out on the bat. Another disappointment was that the bat only came out when I was preaching. Isn't that just like the devil?

On the first night of the meeting, we had a difficult time breaking through in the spirit. It was as if there was a barrier between me and the people when I was preaching, and the demons were coming out slowly. When I went back to my hotel room, I cried out to God. I felt like there was no anointing on me, and I thought maybe my husband needed to preach to the people. The devil had spoken, and for a minute I entertained the thought, "This is an Islamic country; maybe they will receive a man better."

All I wanted was to see God's power manifest; I did not care who He used. God's response to me in prayer was not what I expected to hear. The Lord actually rebuked me. He said I was to walk by faith and not by sight. He told me that without faith it was impossible to please Him. He also said that if I knew what was going on in the spirit and what I was really up against, I would begin to praise Him. I stopped crying, dusted myself off and made up my mind to please God.

The Mount Carmel experience was not to prove that Elijah had power over the wicked Queen Jezebel. It was to make an open declaration that the God of Elijah had power over satan himself. The showdown was not between the prophets of Thailand and me; it was God's battle over all of the powers of darkness. My part was to stand and declare, and God would take care of the light work. The hardest part in warfare is for God to get us to declare His lordship and authority in power. The rest is easy because the devil is no competition for the Most High. The battle was between God and satan; it was a done deal.

All of a sudden a peace came upon me, and setting Eliza free was not the issue anymore. I was more concerned with continuing to lead the people into another realm of worship unto the Lord. On the last night, I walked into the building, and Eliza was sitting in the same seat she had been in all week. Each night she would manifest devils as the word of the Lord went forth. Everyone was used to this, so no one paid her actions any attention. As she sat across from me, we waited for the praise and worship to begin. I felt compelled to walk over and talk to her for the first time. You see, my team had ministered to her up until this time, and I had never personally prayed for her.

I asked her how she was feeling, and she said she was very tired. She told me she slept in the evening when she got off from work because she could not sleep at night. Her boss was a member of the church, and he hired her to help her out. He told me that when she first started working for him, the lights in his office would cut off and on, and the copier would cut on by itself. When he told me this, God reminded me of a strange occurrence that happened the first night of the conference.

There was a sudden surge in the electricity, and the organ started playing by itself while I was preaching. It happened so quickly that my mind talked me out of it. Several people saw it, but no one seemed to be moved. My husband confirmed the occurrence, but we could not explain it, so we left it alone. All of these things came to my remembrance as Eliza shared how she could not sleep at night. I could not explain this feeling, but I felt as if a woman needed to minister personal deliverance to her. It was just a sudden unction of the Holy Ghost. A few minutes before I was about to preach I called the pastor and an interpreter into the office. I invited Eliza to go with me, but she told me she was afraid of me and did not want me to pray for her. I knew I was on the right track.

She began to manifest on the way to the office, so we quickly moved her into privacy. The demons in her began to curse me with foul language in a Chinese tongue. Eliza spoke fluent English, but the demons spoke through her in Chinese. The interpreter told me the demons kept repeating: "Thailand belongs to me. You cannot have Thailand!" When I traveled to China last year it was prophesied that I was called to Thailand. I had only heard of the place in my classes in high school. The Lord also gave me a word in prayer that He would send me to combat the Eye of the Tiger. I searched high and low to find out what this meant. A Chinese psychiatrist we have worked with to study deliverance with his patients finally told me about the Eye of the Tiger.

This term is used to describe one of the highest levels of witchcraft in Asia. Its origination is in Thailand, and it means to do warfare unto the death. I remember a scene in the movie *Rocky* when Sylvester Stallone could not fight anymore. His manager began to yell "Eye of the Tiger" from the corner. He received another burst of energy and won the fight. This is a warfare that is fought by high-level spiritualists who will give their lives for the cause. This is a spiritual warfare through witchcraft. The concept of the Eye of the Tiger is the counterfeit of Revelations 12:11, which says they loved not their lives *unto death*.

Demons are very dumb!

I often share with people the fact that demons are very dumb! They do not think for themselves. They only follow the orders given to them by higher ranking devils. Eliza's bondage was governed by a territorial spirit that ruled over her life from the experience in Thailand. The rulership of the territorial spirit and the sacrifices made in Thailand to satan gave the demons a right to possess her body. I took authority over the principle spirit that ruled over her head in Thailand. I also severed its alliance with the demons that possessed her body. In their stupidity, the demons told on themselves. In the last thirteen years of ministry, I have found this to be the case with severe demonic influence in a person's life. If you reach a wall while ministering deliverance to a person and cannot get a breakthrough, the solution is to wait patiently. The devils will eventually tell on themselves.

Observe the actions of the person or listen to what the demons are making them say. This will usually give you clues on how to pray. The key is that you must be able to discern spirits. The Holy Spirit will let you know if you need to shut the mouth of the devils or listen to what they are saying. There were times in the Bible

111

when Jesus told the spirits to hold their peace, and other times He asked them, "What is your name?" Jesus allowed the demons to speak through the man who was possessed with Legion. (See Mark 5:9.)

After many walls in this deliverance case we finally got a breakthrough. A light was turned on in my head. One breakthrough after another took place. I could tell we had bound the strongman. When the devils in her yelled, "She will have my baby," I knew I had to kill the seed of satan that was on the inside of her. The scripture came to my mind that it is the woman who would bruise the head of the seed of satan. (See Genesis 3:15.) I was the first woman to minister deliverance to this young woman. There are not many female ministers in an Islamic country. Eliza was carrying a demonic Cambion in her belly, and it was my assignment to bruise its head.

Another ruling spirit was the spirit of the vampire. For a second time I asked her why she did not sleep at night. She told me the devil would get her if she went to sleep at night. This explained the manifestations of the night creatures. Her hands took on the form of a scorpion about to attack, and when I rebuked the scorpion spirit, she fell on the ground and started crawling like a snake. I asked the pastor to set her up, and I made the demons allow Eliza to speak. I made a declaration over her head that she would sleep at night and that the devil would not torment her again. I boldly looked into her face and told her to look me into my eyes and tell me who was Lord. I asked her who had more power, Jesus or the devil. It took her a few minutes to say it, but she finally got the words out of her mouth that Jesus had more power than the devil.

I took my hand and put it over the lowest part of her stomach area and cursed the seed of satan from her womb. By the authority of Jesus Christ, I performed a spiritual abortion and killed satan's baby. Her body fell limp as I then called the spirit of Dracula out of her and broke the curse of the living dead off of her. We found out later that she had always been afraid of the dark after becoming obsessed with *Dracula* movies. Eliza shared with the team that when I called out the spirit of Dracula, it increased her faith because she had never told anyone about her obsession with Dracula, which had turned into an uncontrollable fear.

The prophetic ministry is so important in deliverance. It is an encouragement to the person receiving deliverance when they hear a team member calling out something they have never shared. Then they know the Holy Spirit is doing the work. I have nothing against allowing people to write out a list of what they think they need to be delivered from or the generic lists that are already made up. My preference is to flow by the prophetic. We train our teams this way for personal deliverance, but we usually use a generic list for mass deliverance services. Another note is that Eliza did not throw up in a bucket. She was thrown around the room, and she burped a lot. Eliza's manifestations in the pastor's office that night reminded me of my own manifestations when I was first delivered. Demons manifest themselves in many ways:

- The release of air from the body through the mouth or rectum.

- Spitting or vomiting from the mouth.

- Throwing the body of the person violently around the room.

- Speaking through the person or forbidding them to speak.

- Through sweat coming out of the person's pores.

- Through blood coming through the mouth or rectum.

- By changing the person's countenance.

- Through coughing and choking.

- Through crying and the release of tears.

- Through urination or uncontrollable bowel movements.

There are many more, and I must say these are manifestations for milder cases of deliverance. I do not feel led to go into the manifestation of the more serious cases at this time. I also know that there is so much we do not know about deliverance. We are learning more every day. And I must make this statement on the behalf of deliverance ministers everywhere: We are not *exorcists*! My spirit is grieved when people refer to deliverance as an exorcism. The Word of the Lord tells us that this is error.

The seven sons of Sceva were exorcists; demons do not recognize exorcists. The demons declared, "Jesus I know; Paul I know but who are you?" (Acts 19:14–16). Verse 13 tells us that Sceva and his sons were vagabond Jews. The Bible refers to them as exorcists. It also says they took upon themselves to cast out demons by the

Jesus whom Paul preached. The results were that the demons in the man leaped on them, and they left the house naked.

Deliverance ministers must be settled spiritually and physically.

A vagabond moves from place to place and has no physical or spiritual roots. He is unsettled and irresponsible and has a disreputable and questionable lifestyle. Deliverance ministers must be settled spiritually and physically. They must lead lifestyles that are not a reproach among people lest they bring shame to the ministry of Jesus Christ. Last but not least they must be rooted in deliverance to the point of living a well-balanced life with submission to a covering with apostolic authority. Studying the biblical story on the Sceva family leads me to note the following:

↬ There is a difference between exorcism and true deliverance.

↬ A requirement for deliverance ministry is to have a direct relationship with the Lord.

↬ There must be the calling of God on an individual's life to do certain levels of deliverance ministry; people cannot take it upon themselves to jump into this ministry. (The seven sons of Sceva took it upon themselves to call over people who had evil spirits, Acts 19:13.)

↬ Demons do not recognize exorcists; they are only

subject to those under an apostolic mandate.

⇦ The ministry of casting out devils must be accompanied with sound preaching of the gospel of Jesus Christ. The seven sons of Sceva did not preach Jesus, but they wanted to cast out devils.

Deliverance ministry is more than casting out devils. There will be some people who stand before God saying, "Lord, have we not cast out devils in Your name?" Witches and others who are rejected by God can cast out devils. They can command a devil to leave a person because witches can operate by controlling spirits. A controlling spirit uses demons to control people, places and things. The notion that satan cannot cast out satan actually means that true deliverance cannot take place by demonic control. A witch can command a demon to temporarily leave a person, or they can move a spirit to another part of the person's body.

Deliverance ministry ministers to the whole man. Demonic oppression traumatizes a person, and they need more than the devil cast out of them. The same spirits that are cast out of a person are seeking dry places. They are seeking bodies that have been swept clean and garnished. These spirits must have a body to fulfill their mission. It is torment to a devil to wander or have no place to abide. The Bible says we should give no room to the devil. We give him room when the rivers of living waters are not flowing in our lives. When there is no word, there is no water.

Out of our bellies shall flow rivers of living water. This represents the Holy Spirit of God. Without the

Spirit, the Word and the light of God in our lives, we are open to demonic infiltration. The true anointing of deliverance ministry is not just to bring the people out of Egypt and leave them in the wilderness. The power of deliverance ministry is to take the people into the Promised Land. I believe God is raising up a generation that has the grace to lead His people into the Promised Land.

Some ministers would say the things that occur in deliverance ministry are too radical, and it does not take all of that. Many say they do not believe in it. I say those who say this could not have traveled with Jesus. Jesus said if you are not with Him in this ministry, you are not with Him at all.

> He that is not with me is against me; and he that gathereth not with me scattereth abroad.
> —MATTHEW 12:30

Every believer is called to cast out devils.

This is where the line in drawn in ministry. Everyone is not called to spearhead deliverance ministry, but every believer is called to cast out devils. Even if a leader does not feel the call of God to tap into the depths of this realm, he or she should provide an avenue for the people who desire to be delivered. Just as we have every kind of auxiliary you can name under the sun, every church needs a "devil-bustin' auxiliary."

Maybe that name is too radical for your church.

Maybe you can call it an "inner-healing auxiliary." Provide a mechanism that helps people get set free. Whenever Jesus came on the scene, the devils were provoked. The spirits that hid in the temple all the time came out of hiding when the anointing showed up. If you are truly anointed, you will provoke devils, and you need to know how to deal with them.

If you are truly anointed, you will provoke devils.

And to all of the church leaders who may be reading this book, please do not breathe a sigh of relief because devils are not manifesting in your church. This is nothing to sigh about—because *they are there*! They were there when Jesus preached, and they are there when you are preaching, too.

Let us go back to Eliza's deliverance. After the last session with Eliza, when I walked into the sanctuary, there seemed to be a new light in the place. New life breeds new light. I preached on the gifts of the Spirit. As I taught the Malaysian people how to flow in the gifts of God, Eliza sat on the edge of her seat. She could hear what I was preaching, and she was listening enthusiastically, eating up the word of God. Before her deliverance, she slumped in the chair with anguish and torment on her face.

The bat was gone, too! The glory of God was in the place! Deaf ears were opened, epileptic devils were excused from their assignment, but most of all, Eliza was set free! I watched her features transform from what

118

looked like a wild animal into a beautiful young woman. The fear on her face turned into a peace that only those who were present could understand. We went out to dinner at the end of the meeting, and to my surprise Eliza was sitting there as if she had never been bound a day in her life. She was having a normal conversation with my team and me as her face was lit up with Jesus.

She said the pictures of creatures that stayed in her head all the time to torment her mind had gone. The constant pressure on her face and migraine headaches had ceased for the first time since she came to Christ. Eliza was no longer under the bondage of a vampire spirit. I told her to stand on the scripture that God gives His beloved sweet sleep. Eliza still has a lot of ministry ahead of her, and there is much inner healing that needs to take place. The trauma of the demonic experiences she has been through is one of the deepest cases I have ever dealt with.

At the end of the trip I had a better understanding of what God meant when He told me to set my hand-maidens free. Though there were many women in bondage, I believe God sent me to Malaysia especially for Eliza. I must clarify one thing: The church in Malaysia had been ministering to this young woman for thirty months. They had to live with her on a daily basis and deal with all the demonic activity that came along with it. I am in no way trying to take all of the credit for the ministry to Eliza. The fallowed grounds were already broken up when we arrived.

I salute the pastor of this congregation in their great efforts in extending deliverance ministry to a soul in such need. Many pastors would have referred this young lady to a mental institution. God used me and the team from Spoken Word Ministries to water a seed that already had been planted. I am so glad God brought the increase. Now Eliza is sitting like the man from the tombs in the Bible—*clothed and in her right mind!* I am sure the prophets of Thailand are cutting themselves as they have been put to open shame again. Bless the name of the Lord!

God is raising up a generation that will seek His face unconditionally. Their hands and hearts will be free from idols, and the repercussions of this will be blessings. Jesus is a rewarder of those who diligently seek Him.

> But without faith it is impossible to please him: for he that cometh to God must believe that he is, and that he is a rewarder of them that diligently seek him.
>
> —HEBREWS 11:6

It is an honor for me to share another demon-busting testimony all the way from the jungles of Malaysia. To God be all the glory, honor and praise!

Chapter VII

THE PROSPERITY
OF POSTERITY

The devil comes to steal, kill and destroy. As I look back, I recognize all the things the enemy manifested in my life to hinder my purpose in Christ. Although I was from God, the devil must have seen something in my life to fight me the way he did. As I have grown to know the Lord and have endured the attacks of the enemy, it is easy for me to come to the conclusion that the enemy is not very smart. He is not creative because he is not the creator. He operates in the same patterns all the time.

If we studied the devil like he studied us, we would have a better idea of his personal vendetta against us. I know many believers say we do not need to pay the devil any attention as long as we have Jesus. The truth is, God has given us power over the enemy. That power is delegated authority. As I consider the word *delegate* it brings two words to my mind: *representative* and *responsibility*. Not only are we called to represent Jesus in the earth realm, but we have a responsibility to Him.

Responsibility has two very important ingredients:

↝ Burden—a duty or bearing of a load

↝ Accountability—answerable or to be able to give an account.

We are stewards for the Lord. The Bible declares that one day we will have to give God an account of how we fulfilled our responsibilities. It is the job of the enemy to rob us of the things God has given us to do. Remember: The devil comes to steal, kill and destroy. This is his job. If he did not do these three things, he would not be the devil. His essence is robbery, death and destruction.

It is the job of the enemy to rob us of the things God has given us to do.

The enemy wants to distract us with the "Why me blues." Things are coming against you because God has chosen you. The devil has been fired, and you have been hired to take his place! One of my favorite scriptures has always been Proverbs 6:31. It says that if you recognize a thief, you can make him give back what he stole seven times. When I came into the body of Christ, I experienced great compensation in my life. Even today, thirteen years after my conversion, I am experiencing back pay that I could have never imagined.

The curses of the fathers follow us from three to four generations.

I have always noticed the pattern the enemy takes in an individual's life through generational curses. I am a living witness that the generational blessings are greater. The curses of the fathers follow us from three to four generations. The same scripture reveals that thousands shall also receive mercy from this curse. The requirement to receiving this mercy is repentance and obeying God's commandments.

> Thou shalt not bow down thyself to them, nor serve them: for I the LORD thy God am a jealous God, visiting the iniquity of the fathers upon the children unto the third and fourth generation of them that hate me; and shewing mercy unto thousands of them that love me, and keep my commandments.
> —EXODUS 20:5–6

I accepted Jesus Christ into my life when I was twenty-seven years old. By that time I had lived the life of a fifty-year-old woman. I grew up very fast and was always ahead of my age group. It was quite a shock for me to realize the sins I had committed affected my children. I had lived such a rugged life. Surely if the things I did brought curses upon my seed, my children were in trouble. It was a comfort to me to know that it was not too late.

My son Michael was the only child I bore while in the world. All of my other children were born under the covering of powerful intercession with godly lifestyles to back it up. I realize that the devil has an assignment against all of our children. When the woman gave birth to the child in the Book of Revelation, the dragon was stationed in front of her waiting to devour the child at birth. (See Revelation 12.)

The devil has an assignment against all of our children.

Michael seemed to be a calm child. I was a very carnally minded person, so to me he was the picture–perfect child. I had no discipline or gauge in my life. We did whatever we felt like doing as a family. I was a single mother in the military when I took responsibility of rearing my own child. The first door-opener to the devil in my son's life was that he did not live with me for five years in his younger days. Michael lived with his paternal grandparents from age two to seven years old. I gave birth to him when I was eighteen, and the first night he came home from the hospital he slept in the bed with his grandmother.

I thought it was a good thing at the time because I was young, and I just wanted to rest and recover. But I missed out on the bonding that should have taken place between us. To make matters worse I had a very foul mouth and a distorted conception of what family life was all about. My mother cursed me out (in love), so I did the same thing to Mike. In my household it was nothing for an adult to call us over and say things like, "Give me a kiss you little #*@ #." That was the best way they knew how to show love and the best way we knew how to receive it. I can remember sitting down and watching X-rated stand-up comedians such as Dolamite, Richard Pryor and Redd Fox with my son while we laughed and ate popcorn. These men exploited women with the most vulgar language one could imagine.

I was also obsessed with worldly music and club-hopping. These things were priorities in my life, and my son had to fit in with the program. I loved my child, but I could only love him to the extent that love was a reality to me. I was never hugged and kissed and told, "I love you," in my environment. Not only was it not in my home, but I also never witnessed it at many of my friends' homes.

The generational curses of our bloodlines are the enemies of our posterity.

Now that I am saved and filled with God's Spirit, I realize a person cannot give what they do not have. It is important that we impart to our children so godly posterity will be released to future generations. The generational curses of our bloodlines are the enemies of our posterity. We know that a righteous man leaves an inheritance to his children.

A good man leaveth an inheritance to his children's children: and the wealth of the sinner is laid up for the just.

—PROVERBS 13:22

The inheritance that we leave to our seed is much deeper than a life insurance policy, houses or land. The physical, material, financial and spiritual blessings of God should be stored up for our children and their children.

Blessings of God should be stored up for our children and their children.

Our mentality should not be for us to make it in life. After this life we should be able to be a witness to the fullness of our posterity. In another section of this book I talked about the downfall of Joseph. Egypt changed Joseph's heart toward God because he partook of Pharaoh's portion. Daniel reigned in Babylon, but he did not partake of the king's portion, and the Bible says Daniel's countenance was fairer and fatter than the children who ate of the king's portion. (See Daniel 1:15.)

Joseph's countenance changed. He dabbled in the arts of Egypt and got off track. This is in no way to bring discredit to the ministry of Joseph. But I believe the Bible told the whole truth, and we should not pick out the parts that make our flesh feel good. People need to know the success and downfall of men and women of God. If we paint a picture that everything will always be all right and on track, we will only discourage many.

People who have fallen need to know they are not alone. They need to know they can get back up. I believe God allowed the whole story of Joseph to be in the Bible to teach a lesson: We all fall short of the glory.

Proverbs 24:16 says a righteous man falls down seven times, but he will get up every time. The bottom line is: Joseph was a righteous man who fell. There are many more like him throughout the Bible. When Joseph said, "Get my bones out of Egypt," this was a sign that he had gotten back on track with God. In Joseph's testimony to his brothers, he clearly testified of his true assignment to Egypt. There was a time of great famine in the land during his reign. If we look at this picture from a natural standpoint, we would think God's overall concern was the prosperity of His people. Spiritually speaking, it was posterity that God was concerned about.

Genesis 45:7–8 says, "And God sent me before you to *preserve you a posterity in the earth*, and to save your lives by a great deliverance. So now it was not you that sent me hither, but God: and he hath made me a father to Pharaoh, and lord of all his house, and a ruler throughout all the land of Egypt."

Most people think only about fulfilling the vision of God in their lifetime.

God sent Joseph to Egypt to preserve the posterity of his bloodline in the earth. Most people think only about fulfilling the vision of God in their lifetime. David's vision was to build the house of God, but God told him He would not allow him to fulfill the vision because he had shed too much blood. The Lord said He would use Solomon, who would be a man of peace, to complete the vision. God used David's seed to continue his posterity.

> Assuredly Solomon thy son shall reign after me, and he shall sit upon my throne in my stead; even so will I certainly do this day.
>
> —1 KINGS 1:30

One plants, another waters, but it is God who brings the increase. A lifetime of one man is not big enough to fulfill the overall vision. This is why God tells us to be fruitful and multiply. Our seed is called to carry the burden of the vision of God. It is not as hard as the devil tries to make it seem. Jesus' burden is light, and His yoke is easy. Our children just have to be spiritually in place to walk in the promise. Michael is the child who was born out of wedlock, but God always reminds me that he is the child of promise. God does not love one of my children any more than the others, but they do not all have the same calls on their lives.

A lifetime of one man is not big enough to fulfill the overall vision.

When I think of the life Michael (we call him Mike Mike) has lived, I understand why God refers to him as the child of promise. He is the one who the devil is always trying to kill. He is the one who has always been in trouble. He is the one the devil has kept me on my face about. Most Christian families have a child of promise. The world calls them the "black sheep" of the family. We should begin to call these sons and daughters our miracle children of promise. We should not be too blind to recognize the fact that where sin abounds, grace does much more abound! The more trouble the devil releases toward your child, the more grace the Holy Spirit of God releases above that.

Where sin abounds, grace does much more abound!

It was not until I came out of the kingdom of darkness that I realized my son was not very fond of me. When I stepped into the marvelous light, I realized how much God had to do in me. When you live in darkness, the god of this world blinds your mind. But when you come into the marvelous light, you realize the deception you have been walking in. I thought my son was happy with the new conversion. It was my vision to lay everything down and serve Jesus with my whole heart. Mike understood the reality of the devil at a very young age. The enemy would torment him in the midnight hour so much that I slept in the bed with him until he was thirteen years old.

Mike accepted Jesus into his heart. He did not want to be an outright heathen any more. He also had a general fear of God and respected the Holy Spirit. The thing I did not understand was that even though he was not the one who smoked crack and prostituted, the curses I struggled with had rested upon his head. Mike and I did not have the kind of relationship that allowed him to share his thoughts and struggles. I thought we did because we spent so much time together, but today I realize that spending time together does not solidify a relationship.

It is not how much you are together that counts, but what you do when you are together. We need quality time with our children. This will open the lines of communication with them, and we can speak more powerfully in their lives than the devil. When we are distracted by other things in life and do not give our children the attention they need, the devil gives them his attention. Today I realize the things that were important to Michael were never important to me. I was so distracted that I felt he was excited about everything I was excited about.

When we ... do not give our children the attention they need, the devil gives them his attention.

I was saved and delivered from the streets, but there were many basic life principles I could not get a grip on. In my relationship with my child, I felt as if I were shadowboxing with an enemy I could not see. I thought surely he should see the difference in me and want to change, too. We set a standard in our home and lived by it. It was outside of the home that the devil wreaked havoc in my son's life. By his teen years, Mike was so rebellious he started spending the night with one of his friends around the corner from my house on a frequent basis.

God gave me instructions to maintain a standard in my house.

The Lord began to give me, my husband and church members visions of Michael's rebellion. In my prayers, alarms began to go off concerning his soul. God gave me instructions to maintain a standard in my house. At first, I did not have the specifics of what he was actually doing, but I knew that whatever it was, it could not be done in my house. Many saints make the mistake of allowing their children to compromise with things like worldly music and other mind-blinders satan uses against our seed. The scripture stayed in my mind, "As for me and my house, we will serve the Lord" (Joshua 24:15).

The manifestations of Mike's bondage became more prevalent as time went on. This was one of the greatest messes I had in my saved life, and I cried out for a miracle from God. Anyone who knew me personally knew that my oldest son was on the road to destruction. I began to have visions of him in caskets, and God began to show me what I was up against. God does not always show us the good; sometimes He will reveal to us what the devil is trying to do.

I did not pray and ask God to spare his life. God was not the one trying to kill him! I began to do warfare against the spirit of death. I personally took authority over the Grim Reaper himself and forbid him to take my child's life. During the height of Mike's rebellion, the son of one of my best friends was killed in a drug transaction. Her best friend's son was killed on the streets a few months before that. My friend's name was Charlotte, and her son had three beautiful little babies.

A young man who was a close associate of her son became the godfather of these children as part of a vow to look after his dead friend's children. He gave his life to the Lord at Charlotte's son's funeral. Though he came up to the altar, he did not walk away from the lifestyle he was living. In less than a year after Charlotte's son's funeral, this young man's body lay in a casket at his own funeral service. He was hanging out Uptown (I talked about this area in my book *Against All Odds*) in a pool room a few blocks away from where my brother and grandfather were murdered before I got saved.

This young man was told to get down on the floor during a robbery. The assailants warned him not to lift his head. He lifted his head, and they blew it off with a high-powered weapon.

The spirit of death seemed to grip the black communities of Jacksonville, Florida. The most difficult thing for me to do was to look into the eyes of these saved mothers who had lost their sons in cruel street murders. These women all believed God to deliver their sons from the world system of the streets. I know for a fact that Charlotte is one the most fasting and praying women I know. The fruit of her lifestyle also backs up every word she prays. Do I have an explanation for why this happened? No, and I do not believe anyone does! Bad things happen to godly people. I do know that the Word tells us to have faith in God. We must walk by faith and not by sight.

There are times when I have cried out to God because things were not going my way. He firmly rebuked me and told me to get up and walk by faith. With young people dying all around me, I had no choice but to go another level in my faith. The thing that blessed me most was that Charlotte shook herself off and began to pray for my son. She told me the devil had stolen her son, and she would fight with me for mine. That is the *agape* love of Christ. She did not get mad with God because it was her son and not mine. As she faced the greatest challenge she will probably have in her life, she allowed God to use it to take her to the next level.

When her son died, she was not doing warfare the way she is doing it now. Currently she is one of the most dedicated warfare intercessors I know. She is a demon-buster and a great asset to the body of Christ. The trial for her son's murder has not started yet, and God has already strengthened her to endure it.

Mike began to get very bold with his activities. The bolder the devils got in him, the bolder I allowed the Holy Ghost to get in me. One night I was laying hands on his bed at about 3 A.M. I was rebuking the spirits of the streets and taking authority over the generational curses that were released from my past to his present. Mike walked into the door that night and almost ran from my presence. The anointing was on me so heavy I began to prophesy about what he had been doing that night and that God was not pleased.

He fearfully ran into his room and went to sleep. A few days later, he came to me and told me that he had tried marijuana, and he liked it. Though this may have been a tragedy for many mothers, I considered it a breakthrough for me. I knew what I was dealing with. Mike was hanging out with a group of guys who were under the bondage of Rastafarian or reggae spirits. These were the fruits of this spirit:

↬ Dread-lock hair

↬ Cars with booming sound systems and expensive rims

↬ Loud, demonic music

↬ Strong marijuana usage

↬ Attention-getting jewelry and a mouth full of gold teeth (with vampire fangs)

↬ The spirit of mammon and a desire to get money by any means possible

I called the parents of one of the young men I knew Mike was hanging out with. They were saved, and I met with them to explain what was going on with our children. We lay out on our faces and cried out to God on the behalf of our children. We prayed the prayers in my warfare manual and agreed to walk in faith.

God began to give me specific words concerning my son in dreams and visions. I will never forget this dream: I was walking into the club I met Michael's father in. It was called "The Mark V" at the time. As I went into the door, someone cut a lock of my hair out of my head.

I called some of the intercessors in my church who had come out of witchcraft, and they told me that the warlock who taught them witchcraft owned that club. They also told me it was a Rastafarian club. A few weeks later, friends shared with me that they had seen Mike hanging out at the same club. I do not believe it was by chance that Michael's father used to sell drugs on the same corner as a young boy.

Things were coming together. The year before all of these events began to occur, I was involved in spiritual conflict with a group of Rastafarian warlocks, and we put them to open shame. They were calling my house and singing war chants over my phone. They were in direct contact with this club. God showed me that my son had purchased marijuana that was laced with witchcraft from this group of Rastas. They are not regular drug dealers. They pray to certain gods to increase the power and the sales of their drugs in the lives of their customers. They bewitch the buyers to believe that no other dope is like theirs. The spirits honor their sacrifices, and another level of demonic anointing comes upon the drugs.

My son began to look and act like the enemies I had come up against for so many years. He totally rebelled against me and my husband. The devil made him think we were his greatest enemies. My prayer life went to another level as I began to petition God not to allow my son to be comfortable in his state. God's grace was extended toward my family. Mike was at least in a place that he could hear us. After much warfare, we were finally getting a breakthrough.

During the time when it seemed like the devil was winning the battle, I began to receive more and more visions from God. I drew from the prophetic words that were spoken about Mike, and I declared that God was not a man that He should lie. I believed the words of the prophets. I will never forget a prophetic word Mike received when he was about eight years old. He was in a church service in Germany playing during the sermon in the back of the church. The prophet had him and another young man stand up in the midst of her message. When we thought she would rebuke them, she prophesied.

The word to Mike was that he would be a professional football player and do very well at the game. A few years later Pastor Sirretta, who ministers with me at Spoken Word, dreamed that Mike had a scholarship at Florida State University and went into the NFL. Athletics have always been my background, and when I got saved God commanded that I walk away from track and field in the height of my career. He promised that my seed would pick up where I left off. As the state of my son's soul seemed to worsen, God gave me a powerful dream.

I saw a scorpion run under a rug. I was the only one who saw the scorpion run under the rug. People were walking across the rug with lackadaisical attitudes. As I looked at the rug, it began to grow larger and larger. It grew like a large mountain about to erupt. I thought, How big will this scorpion be when it is revealed? As I stood trembling before what I thought was the biggest enemy I had ever faced, the rug was supernaturally flung back. It was not a large scorpion that I saw at all. It was the hand of God. God's hand was so big. I knew it was God because it was full of light. God had the little scorpion in his hand, and He flung it far away from me.

God encouraged me with this dream. He let me know that the devil was the god of deception and magnification. God showed me that He takes what the devil means for evil and turns it around. The devil may start things, like the scorpion running under the rug. But when it looks like the devil is having his way, God is behind the scene running things, and He has the last say. The devil may be the initiator, but God is the creator. The devil is an instigator; he starts stuff! It is always important to remember that God is the creator of anything that the devil has started. I will never forget that little scorpion in the mighty hand of God. In our sight, the attacks of the enemy seem so great, but when we put our problems in God's hand, they become as a speck of dust. Hallelujah!

God is behind the scene running things, and He has the last say.

I began to get small breakthroughs with Michael. It started when he began to spend time at home. He looked like a mess. His hair was sticking all over his head. He had a rack of gold vampire teeth in his mouth, and he wore his clothes inside out. It took everything in me to get past what I saw. The devil had turned my child into everything I preached against. I am sure my enemies were laughing at me, but I had the assurance that God would have the last laugh. My son has always been athletic, but the curse of "almost" ruled over his head. This is the same curse that plagued me in my younger days. The devil would only let me go so far. If it was not a pulled muscle that held me back, a crazy boyfriend got in my way.

Michael was about to graduate from high school with no hope of a scholarship. He had put his trust in a coach who did not have his best interest at heart. I tried to get Mike to go to the high school I attended because I knew the coaches would look out for him there. Again, Michael rebelled! By the grace of God I was able to get Michael into Grambling University on a scholarship with Coach Eddie Robinson, who is a legend in college football. I mailed Michael's videos to him, and he liked what he saw. Michael's high school coaches did not celebrate his achievement and only made matters worst by telling him he would never make it in football. They said he was not good enough.

But I had an eye in the natural and in the spirit. Michael had what it took! I just had to convince him to get past all the negative words he had heard from those who could not see the vision. Michael's heart's desire was to play in the NFL, but his chances in the natural seemed so far away. Michael's grades were so bad in high school that he had to enter Grambling under the Prop 40 program, a plan to help young people get into college on athletic scholarship by giving them an opportunity to raise their grade point average.

Michael maintained a 3.0 average that year at Grambling. Everything was going well until the coaching staff changed, and the new regime did not know Mike and made no promises of a scholarship. When the new coach told me that the Mike's chances of a scholarship under his leadership were slim, I told him that I would take my son to Florida State University. The coach said I was crazy. Florida State would not even look at my son. The Lord told me to bring Mike home for a year. I enrolled him in a local junior college and took him to the track coach with the same line I used when I walked into Mount Hood Community College twenty years ago.

I asked the coach if he would give my son a scholarship if he beat all of his athletes running. Who could turn such an offer down? Mike obtained a full scholarship for one year. I was then led to contact the head track coach at Florida State University. They watched Michael at the junior college and noted the potential he had. The transition from football to track was not easy for Michael. He had only one year of track experience in high school. He walked on the track team one week before the regional meet and qualified for the state championship. With no training, he finished third in the 400 meters in the entire state of Florida. This was impressive, but it was not enough to compete on the NCAA level.

The coaches finally told Mike that if he could complete twenty-six credit hours in one semester and graduate from junior college, they would give him a chance at a scholarship. With the help of a good family friend, Michael completed all the courses with the highest grade point average ever recorded at the college for that amount of hours. I thank God for Mr. Charles. He helped Michael with administrative and tutoring needs. Without him it would have been almost impossible. I know that God sent him our way for such a time as he did. Michael was accepted at Florida State University on a partial scholarship and quickly became the second fastest quarter-miler to attend the college. The only runner who ran a time faster than his was the great Olympic runner Walter McCoy.

The coaches told Mike that if he ran below a 46.0 time in the quarter they would put him on scholarship. Michael achieved that goal and was then told he would be put on full scholarship if he qualified for the NCAA Championships. Michael qualified for the NCAA Championships, but his success was interrupted suddenly. Though Michael appeared to be prospering on the outside, the generational curses of my bloodline plagued his inner being. I did not know he was still smoking marijuana, and he had so many speeding tickets the police department knew him by first name.

Michael ignored the rules. He provoked the police with his appearance and loud music. He had no reverence for the law, and his disrespect for authority soon caught up with him. My intercessors were having dreams and vision of Michael getting in big trouble. My husband and I both had alarms in our spirits that something was about to go down. Finally, reality hit me in the face when I got a phone call that Michael was in jail. We paid the bail and got him out, and by the time I had paid the first bail he was arrested several other times. He had been to jail so many times that the inmates in Duval and Leon counties knew him well. Michael called me from jail one day and told me he felt as though he was getting used to being locked up. Somehow Mike never missed his classes and always made track practice.

My son was on the way to disaster, so I began to change the way I prayed for him. I asked God to remove the grace that was over Mike's head but to spare his life. I had a very effective prison ministry, but I was not willing to let the devil give me one to my son. While visiting home over the Christmas holidays, Michael got arrested for disturbing the peace with his car system. My son was not robbing, killing and selling drugs. He was running red lights, speeding and playing his music too loud in the public. This was a "mischievous" spirit. I knew the assignment was not against Michael, but against me. He became everything I preached against.

When Michael was arrested in my city, it was too much for me to bear. The Lord allowed me to visit him at midnight on a special pass. I entered the private visitation room praying and prophesying. He sat there with his hair twisted all over his head looking like he had stuck his finger in an electric plug. His teeth were shining with a gold and diamond rack in his mouth. I demanded that he take the cosmetic removable gold teeth out of his mouth. I gave him an ultimatum—the teeth or no bail! My heart weakened as I saw the bondage in his eyes that showed me that he had a soul tie with this object. He refused to take the teeth out of his mouth. He chose to stay in jail rather than to give up those gold vampire teeth.

As I walked away from him, he finally gave me the teeth. It took everything in him to do it. By the time Michael got back to school, he had another warrant for his arrest in that county for a traffic violation. He had to turn himself in. I tried to bail him out this time, but things had changed. Michael was now listed as a repeat offender and was facing felony charges. I was forced to get a lawyer. My heart almost failed when they told me he was being offered a five-year minimum sentence. Michael's facial expressions were more serious this time. This was no longer a passing fad. He was about to become a convicted felon.

Everyone told me I needed to let him learn a lesson, but God was not saying the same thing to me. He told me to stand in the gap, and He would deliver my son and keep his name clean. I will never forget the night that I went to Michael's court date. I drove over two hours down a dark interstate on Halloween night at midnight. It seemed such an evil time. The enemy tried to tell me that he failed to get me while I was in Tallahassee attending Florida State, but that he would surely have my son.

I did warfare that night! As day broke, I stood at the courthouse with a bottle of anointing oil in my purse. I anointed my hands and the bottom of my feet. I laid hands on every place I could touch. I claimed the scripture that wherever the soles of my feet would tread, the land belonged to me.

> Every place that the sole of your foot shall tread upon, that have I given unto you, as I said unto Moses.
>
> —JOSHUA 1:3

To God be the glory! Michael was given sixty days of night jail. The judge allowed him the go to track practice and school in the daytime. He checked into jail every night at 6:30 PM. He had no car because his driver's license was taken from him. Every evening he sat on the bench outside of the jail waiting to be let in. He would call me to pray with him before he was locked down. They released him at 5 A.M. every morning.

Though the results were a blessing from the Lord, Mike still had many challenges. He was sleeping next to some mentally insane and hard-core criminals. Tallahassee is known for having a tough jail system in every aspect of the word. By the time Michael reported to do his time, my book *Against All Odds* was distributed throughout the facility. God gave me favor with some of the staff, and they gladly allowed the books to be distributed throughout the population. Michael often complained of the loud sirens from surprise drills and strip downs in the middle of the night. He still had to go to school the next day like a normal student and return to his cell to be locked up at night.

Michael got out ten days early for doing good time, but most importantly he came out a new man. Michael stepped on the track and ran the fastest times he had ever run. It could have only been the grace of God. Mike only lost a portion of his scholarship support, but he was still allowed to compete for the season. He did fall behind on his grades, but the athletic department promised to restore his status when he got back on track. And get back on track is exactly what he did! Michael improved his study habits and became focused. The New Year's Eve after this dilemma, he rededicated his life to Jesus Christ. As I was releasing my CD *Devil, Boo I See You*, we had a massive altar call.

My son was the first one at the altar. God had taken me through another mess, but it was worth the miracle!

The thing that brings joy to my heart is seeing how this mess has brought Michael and me so much closer than before. If the princes over Tallahassee had only known! Michael had seen the Lord move mightily on his behalf. He had to have a mess so Jesus could give him a miracle. The Lord allowed the enemy to come in like a flood so He could raise the standard in Mike's life! God made the steel that formed to war in his life. Therefore, no weapons formed against him could prosper.

Michael had given up all hope to play NFL football. I continually reminded him of the prophecy that was given to him when he was eight years old. A woman picked him out of a large crowd and said that he would be an NFL player. Michael always loved football, but obstacles always hindered him from playing. He was doing very well in track and field, and his coaches had convinced him that football was a pipe dream. In the deepest part of my inner being, I knew that this boy was made to play in the NFL for God's glory.

The Lord allowed me to pastor and provide ministry for many NFL players, and I began to have strong burden in this area. Nothing was lining up with the words that had been spoken over Mike's life. I kept telling people that my oldest son was going into the NFL in 2002, his last year at Florida State University. Finally he got the courage to leave the track team and try out for football, but his grades were a disaster.

During the time Michael worked out with the team, he stood out from the rest like a diamond in the rough.

The seed was implanted in his mind that he really could play football. This only made matters worst in Michael's mind. He knew that he could play, but because of his grades there was no opportunity for him to prove himself.

I preached personal sermons to Mike. I reminded him of God's promise to me. I told him how I had given up my track career for the gospel, and God promised that my seed would pick up where I left off. I asked him if he thought it was by chance that he had a scholarship at the same university I attended. Though Michael heard my words, the obstacles before him had an even louder voice. Michael sincerely began to make efforts toward God, but the peer pressure was so great.

Ardell and I also have a younger son named Ardell who attends West Point. He was given a football scholarship the same year Michael was to graduate. Our younger son was given an opportunity to travel to the Army-Navy Game as a freshman on the roster. Ardell and I arrived at the game not understanding that the Holy Ghost was about to drop the bomb. Secret Service vehicles scanned the facility. This was the largest football game in the country! We had no idea. The president of the United States tossed the coin. I had prayed with Ardell the night before. He asked God to let him play and get so many yards. I remember sternly correcting him saying: "Touchdown, boy. We are believing God for a touchdown!"

Within a few minutes after the kickoff, Ardell had run a sixty-yard touchdown in front of a crowd of seventy thousand people. The commentators called his name over and over again. This was more than Ardell's mind could handle. He was happy just to be on the plane with the team, and now his name was ringing over the stadium. The enemy even attempted to shut him down with an ankle injury before the first half was over. Ardell's dad and I touched and agreed in the stands for his supernatural recovery and that he would be awarded MVP of the game. God showed up and showed out! As the commentators yelled, "It is a miracle; Daniels is back on the field!" I could only give God the glory.

God showed up and showed out!

As Ardell sat behind the table at the press conference as a freshman MVP of the largest football game in the nation, I know all of heaven was watching. Meanwhile, Michael was watching Ardell on national television, and something sparked on the inside of him. Mike Mike knew Ardell had sold out to Jesus. The spirit of the Lord came on me a few weeks later, and I prophesied to my son in my living room. The Lord said unto him: "Son, if you would sell out to Me, I will sell out to you. I will not only allow you to go into the NFL, but I will make you the best at what you do. Surrender to Me, and you will be known as one of the fastest men in the world."

As I prophesied to my own son, it seemed as if he did not hear a word I said. By faith I walked off and believed that not one word fell to the ground. My husband and I continued to intercede on Mike's behalf, and we gave his situation to the Lord.

Michael began to press hard toward his academics.

The Lord allowed him to major in sports management, and one of his teachers was a scout for the NFL. It would seem that this would be the avenue for Mike to get his big break, but this was too easy for God. Most of the time, He takes His people the long way around! Michael, with his lackadaisical personality, never mentioned to his teacher that he could play football. Everyone knew Mike as a track runner. They did not know he had hands that could catch a hot potato.

Michael tried out for the NFL at the Pro Day Trials at Florida State University. He ran with some of the greatest wide receivers in the nation. Michael ran a 4.30 forty-meter dash on wet grass. Not only was it the fastest time in the field, it is one of the fastest times in the NFL with good conditions. The word of the Lord that was spoken over his life tarried, but this was a sign that it would come to pass. A couple of teams took interest in Mike because of his fast time but made no real efforts to contact him. On NFL Draft Day, Michael finally received a phone call. It was from a major squad in California. They verbally invited him to a camp to tryout but never followed upon the call.

Michael appeared discouraged. I continued to minister the word of the Lord. I called his attention to Isaiah 49, which promises that those who wait on the Lord will not be put to shame. I told Michael to meditate on this scripture day and night. One of the NFL players God has called me to pastor called and told me that his wife had a dream that Mike was signing an NFL contract. What an encouragement this witness was at the time. The draft was over, the camps had started, and Mike was on his way home from college.

I was on the road preaching as my son came home from college with a bachelor's degree in sports management. I told him not to worry about the graduation ceremony because the Lord had shown me he would have a phone call that would not allow him to attend. The week Mike was supposed to march down the isles of the Florida State University commencement ceremony, he was called to report to the Jerry Rice training camp. My soul rejoiced as I flew home for one day to put him on that plane to California. After one day of training with the legendary Jerry Rice, Michael was invited to try out with the Oakland Raiders and the San Francisco 49ers. The first team to see Mike signed him for his first NFL contract on the first day of the trial. Which team was it? Do you really have to ask? God promised that my son would pick up where I left off.

God is the master of turning a mess into a miracle!

Mike was given an award as the best athlete in track and field at Florida State for the year 2002. He was signed in California by the San Francisco 49ers. I attended Florida State in college and ran for the Army in San Francisco. I trained in San Jose. Not only does Michael play in San Francisco and practice in San Jose, but he also trains on the same track I practiced on many years ago. The generational curse was broken, and Michael is on the trail of my generational blessing. Do not try to figure it out. God is the master of turning a mess into a miracle!

As I have matured in the Lord, I have learned that our main focus should not be on developing a prosperity mentality. As long as our minds are focused on the posterity of our seed, prosperity is inevitable. It is not just about us and our immediate environments. God wants us to plant seeds in our lifetime that will affect our seed for a thousand generations. I am a living witness; the generational blessings will outrun the curses every time.

As long as our minds are focused on the posterity of our seed, prosperity is inevitable.

Chapter VIII

DEALING WITH OUR ROOTS

As I sit in my bed, my mind is stayed on the fact that God has made us in such an awesome way. He allowed us to have a personality, a will, and He even gives us choices in life. It amazes me how God has so many gifts in the body. We are individuals with mighty callings on our lives. We are all a part of such a big plan, yet so distinct in the way God has made us. As the people of God, we are so unique in the way He uses us.

Some ministries put heavy emphasis on spiritual warfare, reaching out to the inner city or teaching financial stewardship, with dozens more walking out diverse high callings in other areas. Where am I going with this observation? Every successful kingdom has a common denominator at its foundation. For the people of God, that common denominator is faith.

Without faith it is impossible to please God. That is what the perfecting of the saints is all about in Ephesians 4:12—bringing the saints to a place of maturity as we move toward the unity of faith. The strength of any belief system is the ability of the believers of that system to be in one accord. The Bible says a kingdom divided against itself cannot stand.

> And if a kingdom be divided against itself, that kingdom cannot stand.
>
> —MARK 3:24

Without faith it is impossible to please God.

The word of the Lord also declares that one can put a thousand to flight; two, ten thousand.

> How should one chase a thousand, and two put ten thousand to flight, except their Rock had sold them, and the LORD had shut them up?
>
> —DEUTERONOMY 32:30

In 2 Thessalonians 2:1–3, the Bible tells us not to be shaken in mind or troubled by spirit, word or letter. Breaking this scripture down in the Greek, this verse can be paraphrased: Do not be moved by intellect or human nature (mind). Also, do not let demonic attacks (spirit), the truth of the word (*logos*) or religious spirits (letter) trouble you.

The strength of any belief system is the ability of the believers...to be in one accord.

The scripture goes on to say that there must be a falling away first. The word *falling* is very important to note. It is pronounced *apostasia* in the Greek, and it means "to fall away from the truth as to defect or forsake." This is the opposite of the Greek word *apostello*, which means "apostolic or sent ones." To compare these two words, one means "to be sent" and the other means "to run or *fall* away." We are living in a time when many will run away from the truth. The Word says they will have itching ears and not be able to endure sound doctrine.

> For the time will come when they will not endure sound doctrine; but after their own lusts shall they heap to themselves teachers, having itching ears.
>
> —2 TIMOTHY 4:3

They will be like the seed that fell upon stony places, about which Matthew 13:5–6 says:

> They had not much earth because they had no deepness of earth.
> When the sun was up (the heat was on), they were scorched because they had no root.
> They withered (ran) away.

I believe the Lord has been speaking to me consistently about roots because this is the problem many have with their faith. People cannot believe God because of bad roots in their lives. The Lord showed me some things concerning fallow grounds. I saw grounds that were hard, cold, barren and inactive. The top of the ground was parched, but it was what I saw under the ground that really got my attention. Beneath the ground was a huge system of large roots. I heard, "The fallow grounds must be broken up!" I thought, *How? How can fallow ground be broken up with so many larger roots under the ground?*

This is how it is in the spirit realm. The fallow ground of our hearts cannot be plowed because of long-standing root systems that are choking out the truth. These roots forbid the grounds to be cultivated to receive the seed of God's Word. Faith comes by hearing the Word. Matthew 13 speaks of birds that eat up the seed of the word. These birds eat only what is above ground.

The enemy…can only get that which is not implanted, or engrafted, in the ground of your heart.

Only the engrafted word will save our souls. The word *engrafted* in the Greek is *emphutos*, which means "implanted." The *American Heritage Dictionary* defines implanted as "to securely insert into the ground or to embed." It is very difficult for seed to take root on the top of the ground. This is why the fallow grounds must be broken up! All land must be plowed before the planting. The Bible says the enemy comes immediately to steal the seed of the word. He can only get that which is not implanted, or engrafted, in the ground of your heart.

What does "fallow grounds" of the heart actually mean? First look at Jeremiah and his statement concerning this issue. Jeremiah spoke of two things that had to take place concerning the hearts of men. There had to be: (1) a breaking up; and (2) a circumcision or cutting away. Both of these actions referred to the heart and required something sharp to do the job. Hebrews 12 declares that the Word of the Lord is sharper than any two-edged sword. The Word is an excavator. Yes, it imparts, but we must first allow the Word to dig up and clear out the stuff that is not needed.

This is what circumcision does. It cuts off the extra that is not needed. Medical research has proven that men who are not circumcised tend to get infections easier. This is why the human heart must be circumcised by the Word. The heart gets spiritually infected when there is no circumcision. Infection of the body occurs when agents invade it and cause it to operate out of synchronization with its natural system. In like manner, the uncircumcised heart is filled with contamination that will always keep mankind out of synchronization with God.

God put an excavating word in Jeremiah's mouth: "Then the Lord put forth his hand, and touched my mouth. And the Lord said to me, Behold, I have put my words in thy mouth. See, I have this day set thee over the nations and over the kingdoms, to *root out*, and to

155

pull up, and to destroy, and to throw down, to build and to plant" (Jeremiah 1:9–10).

According to this scripture, Jeremiah had to clear the land before he could effectively build. God warned Jeremiah not to be afraid of the faces of the people. This word *faces* in the Hebrew is pronounced *paw-neem*. It is defined as faces that do battle with their countenance. People will not smile at ministers who are speaking words that cut to the heart. In Act 7:54 the Word of the Lord says that when Stephen testified before the council of elders and scribes, the words he spoke cut them to their heart. Stephen addressed them as "stiff-necked" and uncircumcised in heart.

God is raising up warriors in the spirit who will not be afraid of the modern-day *paw-neem*. Today preachers are not pulled out of the city and stoned, but they are persecuted in more modern ways. Because Stephen preached in a way that was not common to them, the elders and scribes accused him of blasphemy. The Bible says Stephen ministered in a way that kept them from resisting the wisdom and spirit he came in. This forced them to set up false witness against him.

Faith will increase in the hearts of the people when the leaders come out of the wilderness of tradition.

Acts 6:14 reveals that they were concerned about the customs Moses had given them. I believe faith will increase in the hearts of the people when the leaders come out of the wilderness of tradition, religion and "how it has always been done." The word *customs* in Acts 6:14 is *ethos*. It means "prescribed manners, habits or conventional ways." Based on this scripture, I can safely say we must be careful not to write prescriptions for solutions that are outdated when it comes to ministry. I realize the Word is the same yesterday, today and forevermore, but with that is the balance that God takes us from one glory to the next.

There was a grace in the wilderness that could not be taken into the Promised Land. The key that opened the door to the ones who could enter the Promised Land was having "another spirit." This was the generation that was "well able." This was the generation that could get past the giants in the land. This was the mountain-moving generation. This was the generation that had dealt with their bad roots—the things that try to follow us into our "promised land."

Let us review Mark 11:20, the passage in which Jesus cursed the fig tree. The Bible says Jesus was hungry, and He noticed the fig tree from afar. After taking a closer look, Jesus saw that the tree had no fruit. Just in passing, He calmly mentioned to the disciples that no one would ever eat of this tree again. No attention was brought to this matter until Peter later noticed that the tree was dried up at the root.

In dealing with demonic roots we must first approach the issue of faith.

Jesus had cursed the tree's ability to reproduce.

Roots are the support system by which a tree is fed. Jesus cut off the tree's provision, stopping its source at the root. You can distinguish a tree by its fruit, but the seed of the fruit is in the root system. Jesus broke up the foundation of the tree's ability to stand. In dealing with demonic roots we must first approach the issue of faith in the story of Jesus and the fig tree.

Matthew 11: 24 clearly states that whatsoever we desire, when we pray, if we believe, we shall receive. On the other hand James said, "You believe that there is one God; you do well because the devils believe and have sense enough to tremble" (James 2:19). These two scriptures provide a formula for faith that cannot be denied. This formula adds up to the fact that faith without works is dead, something James also noted when he wrote, "As the body without the spirit is dead, so is faith without works dead" (James 2:20).

We must ... recognize the things that are not prospering toward the purpose of God in our lives.

Naturally speaking, our bodies cannot function without our spirits in them. We must recognize the same principle that our faith cannot be effective without works. It is like taking a person's spirit out of his body and trying to make him walk. The body is dead without the spirit in it. By faith Jesus cursed the fig tree to the root. The first thing He did was to recognize that the tree was not prospering in its purpose. We must be able to recognize the things that are not prospering toward the purpose of God in our lives and be willing to deal with them.

Without faith it is impossible to please God. It does not take faith to get things out of your life that are not close to you, but it is hard to speak to the mountain when you are in love with it. Sometimes it is hard to see obstacles that stand between us and God when we have soul ties with them. God delivered me from soul ties with man. I was subliminally bound to a leader in my church. I protected him as a leader even sometimes when he was wrong. I did not mean to do it; I simply could not see clearly because of the relationship.

> ## Our dependence on another person ... can become like "another god."

I would often say that every ministry needed a leader like him. I could not see myself operating in ministry without this person because I felt that he was a part of the foundation. It was through much hurt, shame and pain that God excavated these kinds of bad roots out of my life. It is amazing how we can so easily begin to depend on our natural surroundings or the things that have become common to us. God will have no other god before Him. Even our dependence on another person to operate in ministry can become like "another god."

People in the ministry complained to me, but I

could not hear their cry. It was not until God gave me the revelation of "Snake Season" that I even began to understand where they were coming from. After my deliverance from drug addiction and prostitution, I thought I would never feel the grips of the strongman around my neck again. Well, the devil did not come with a spirit from the streets this time. He disguised himself in the form of a "church spirit." It was a spirit I became familiar with, and with all my discerning gifts I could not see it! I could not see this spirit pulling on my marriage, my ministry and everything else in life that was dear to me. If I were not free from it today, I would not even have the breath in my body to talk about it.

Even when the Holy Spirit tugged at my heart, I denied that it was there. In denial, I took this problem on the road with me. I opened doors for this problem and even began to depend upon it. It took all of the Holy Ghost on the inside of me to realize that it was not the assignment of a person, but a spirit determined to take me out. By the time I was able to recognize this spirit, it had me in its grips like a puppet on a string. I thought I was in charge, but "it" was really running things. My only way out was to admit it and quit it. The circumstances were severe because the roots had grown so big. These were underground roots that had never been addressed.

The circumstances were severe because the roots had grown so big.

Through fasting and prayer I allowed the Lord to

cut to the root of my deliverance. I found myself over the bucket getting set free from the thing I feared in the natural more than anything: being close to a snake and not knowing it! In the natural I would always look around in wooded areas in fear that a snake would come upon me by surprise. I could not image a spiritual snake being more detrimental to me. As hard as it was to walk out, this situation has brought unity in my marriage, order in my church and peace to my mind. My husband and I are walking as one like never before.

Sometimes the struggles would get so hard the enemy would try to play tricks on my mind. Today I can stand before Jesus and say that what was once an everyday struggle has become a smooth walk with God. I know the challenges of the life of a demon-buster. Despite this, I could never fathom the strategic placement of so many people around me who were not really for me. Their presence alone caused turmoil in my personal life and put pressure on relationships that were ordained by God. I will never forget that while we were on a forty-day watch during the midnight hour, I heard the Spirit of the Lord say, "Make them walk the plank!" I asked God who He was referring to. He only responded, "The rebels...they are forming a coup against you."

God instructed me to put the sword of the Word to their backs and make them walk the plank. He showed me the scriptures saying, "Rebellion is as the sin of witchcraft" (1 Samuel 15:23). He went on to say a rebel is a witch and that I must deal with the witchcraft in the church. I began to realize that I had been putting my trust in the wrong people. My marriage and ministry were being affected because I was yoking up with the enemy in discussing my personal business. I started noticing that people who were known enemies against our ministry knew my business. The realization was a jolt, but I repented and vowed never to do it again.

When God moved certain individuals out of my life, the problems left.

When God moved certain individuals out of my life, the problems left. Things that I had cried out to God about over the years simply left. They just walked out of the door with the people God moved from around me. The problem I always had to discuss (with the ones I thought I could trust the most) was not there anymore. As it turned out, it was the "ones I thought I could trust" who were the problem in my house. When I got folks out of my business, God showed me myself. He allowed me to embark upon maturity in my relationship with my husband that I could have never thought of in my wildest dreams.

The people I once trusted so much walked out of my life and began to defame my name publicly. They hit my marriage, my ministry and even my children. The things they said really did not bother me because the problem was not in my house anymore. I did not even waste God's time asking Him why. Just as God allowed Sisera to come to Jael's house so that she could kill him, God allowed this thing to manifest itself in the early stages of my ministry so that I could kill it now. I put the hammer to the nail on the head of the enemy and assassinated it. The problem was dead! Hallelujah!

I pray that every leader will take heed to the next chapter. Please know that you do not have to go through all that I have experienced. I know that my autobiography *Against All Odds* had a special anointing to help people coming out of the world. It is my vision that this testimony in *From a Mess to a Miracle* would give light to those who have come into the church. Yes, there are giants in the land, but we are well able! We have nothing to fear but fear it self.

When I got folks out of my business, God showed me myself.

Like Job, the thing that I feared most came upon me. But do not be moved; I also came out of it with double the blessing. It is my prayer that you will learn from my experience if you ever have to walk through a "Snake Season." And if you are walking in the cool of the day with God, eventually you will.

Chapter IX

SNAKE SEASON

The Spirit of the Reptilian

As I walked through the parking lot of my hotel on a hot spring day in Gainesville, Florida, my peace was interrupted by the sight of a small snake running across my path. I avoided the creature by taking a detour to my room. As I walked, the Lord softly spoke to my heart and said, "It is snake season!"

It is natural for snakes to come out of hibernation during the spring in Florida. And though snakes are not my favorite animals, as I came across this one for some reason I remained calm and collected. The Lord began to share with me that whatever we see in the natural realm is a manifestation of what is happening in the spirit. God said unto me, "You have made it through the winter [which represents hard times], and now you have a testimony. The devil wants your testimony. The snakes are coming out of hibernation to take your testimony. Beware of the *reptilian* spirit!"

Whatever we see in the natural realm is a manifestation of what is happening in the spirit.

This word from the Lord prompted me to search the Scriptures concerning this spirit. In Genesis 3:1, satan was depicted as a serpent. Job 40:5 speaks of Leviathan, which represents the devil. The spirit of pride caused Lucifer to fall from grace, and the Book of Job makes reference to a crocodile king of the children of pride. Finally, in Revelation 12:9, the devil is manifested as the Great Dragon.

These are all reptile or reptilian spirits. There are many underground cults that worship the spirit of the reptile, or demons that call themselves "reptilians." The word that the Lord spoke to me began to open up like windows in a computer. As I began to meditate on it, the Lord began to unfold the revelation of "snake season" to me. First he gave me the characteristics of a reptile:

↬ They are cold-blooded animals.

↬ They are usually covered with scales.

↬ They love warm places.

↬ They have thick skin.

↬ They lay eggs.

In studying these characteristics, I compared them to the characteristics of spirits that operate in the church. The definition and biblical reference for each is as follows:

1. **Cold-blooded (Ephesians 4:31).** To be cold-blooded means to be *ectothermic,* or "to change body temperature with the environment." This word also means to execute an action without any heart or emotions. On the streets, a cold-blooded person was considered ruthless and capable of operating with malice. To operate with malice means to have evil intent without cause or reason against a person.

Cold-blooded animals hibernate during the winter and come out when the spring season breaks. God revealed to me that the reason there is so much crime, confusion and revelry during college spring break celebrations is because of the "spirit of the season." In the natural the snakes come out, but there also is a spirit of devilish living that escalates during the break of this season. Devil worshipers and occult followers call it the "spring equinox." This is the season when the fertility gods are worshiped and those that want to release curses plant seed for their harvest. This is the time that spirits are loosed to ignite pornographic activity and sexual orgies. It is the spirit of the party animals whereby everything and anything goes!

I do not think that it is by chance that the timing of Mardi Gras is strategically placed so close to the college spring break celebration. The god of Mardi Gras is Bacchus, the god of partying and revelry. My husband and I ministered to a young man whose parents were ministers of a very successful church. The young man is a very talented gospel recording artist, but he was bound by a strong cocaine addiction. My husband and I fell in love with the young man at first sight. We will call him Jimmy for the purpose of telling his story. We ministered deliverance to Jimmy in our hotel after a meeting that we held on the East Coast. The prophetic anointing of God fell upon me, and I began to prophesy to him.

I told him he had some soul ties with the city of New Orleans that had to be broken. I also explained that God had shown me how a generational curse of death on the streets of this city was set against his life. I said that the spirit of "Bacchus" ruled over his head and that many considered him to be a party animal. He looked at me as if he had seen a ghost and nodded his head to signal that I was right in all that I had said. After one session with him, he went on another bout with cocaine a few weeks later. Things on the streets were pretty rough on him this time. He eventually flew into one of our conferences to spend time with Ardell and me.

For the first time, he shared his story with me about his late uncle. His father's brother had died a homeless alcoholic on the streets of New Orleans. Jimmy explained to me that whenever he tried to leave the city limits, he had an uncontrollable desire to stay. He said he would even have his friends to drop him off at the city limits because something forbad him to leave. The thing that scared him most before he came to join us was an experience he had in an old hotel during Mardi Gras.

He explained that he fell asleep drunk after many days of partying, and his dead uncle came into the room (in a dream) and was calling him to the streets to party some more. He said it was so real that he was awakened in a cold sweat. The prophecy I had spoken to him came alive in his head. It was the prophetic word of God that stuck with him even when the first sessions of deliverance did not. He had never told anyone his secret, but because the Lord had revealed it unto us, he sought deliverance through our ministry again.

As we ministered deliverance, the first thing we accomplished was to sever the soul tie between him and his late uncle. It was this tie in the spirit that held the generational curse that ruled over his head in place. Jimmy is still attending ministry sessions at this time, but his breakthrough has been life changing. To God be the glory!

2. **Scales (Job 41:15; Acts 9:18).** In the Book of Job, the Bible refers to the scales that cover Leviathan, the king of the children of pride. Acts 9:18 speaks of scales that fell from Paul's eyes. Based on these two scripture references, I feel very safe in saying that the scales of the snake represent pride and spiritual

blindness. The Word of the Lord tells us that "pride goeth before destruction" (Proverbs 16:18). The word *destruction* in the Hebrew is pronounced *shay ber*. One of the interpretations of this word is "to tear the view" or to "hurt the interpretation."

Pride distorts our spiritual insight. It is a type of idolatry through which we put ourselves before God. Lucifer fell to this spirit. He said, "I will exalt myself!" Pride exalts "self," and when "self" is exalted, God is put down. This destruction destroys a person's perception of what God is saying because the person takes his attention off God and puts it on himself.

Pride distorts our spiritual insight.

Lucifer was the most beautiful creature God created. But when he brought attention to himself, he ultimately fell. In the next scene, we see him in the garden as a snake. I have known great warfare intercessors whom God used in awesome ways to succumb to the spirit of pride because of the gift of God on the inside of them. When I tried to pull their coattails and tell them to slow down, they resisted me. They said they heard from God for themselves. I was the one who taught them warfare and intercession, and all of a sudden they outgrew me.

These intercessors left the ministry and eventually turned back to lifestyles of drug addiction and everything that goes along with it. Leviathan manifests itself in the neck of the person; Job 41 says Leviathan's strength is in his neck. This bring me to the subject of the next characteristic of a reptile; it has thick skin.

> For I know thy rebellion, and thy stiff neck: behold, while I am yet alive with you this day, ye have been rebellious against the Lord; and how much more after my death.
>
> —DEUTERONOMY 31:27

3. **Thick skin.** To have thick skin means to be hard to penetrate or reach. A person with a stiff neck is one who also is hard to reach. Moses told the people that he recognized their rebellion. First Samuel 15:23 says "rebellion is as the sin of witchcraft, and stubbornness is as iniquity and idolatry." The greatest manifestation of "thick skin" is stubbornness. A stiff neck, thick skin, stubbornness, iniquity, idolatry, rebellion and witchcraft are all manifestations of an ill will toward the things of God and represent spiritual assignments against God's people.

4. **Warm places (Matthew 12:43).** This scripture reveals that demons that are cast out of people roam around seeking dry places. The word *places* in the Greek is *an oo dros*. This word means "waterless and having no spirit." It actually means that demons seek out lukewarm places. Just as snakes seek warm places to hibernate in the natural, demons seek

places (preferably human bodies) to hibernate in.

Revelation 18:2 mentions a habitation of devils. The word *habitation* is *katoiketerion* in the Greek. It is defined as a dwelling place or permanent house to abide in. God wants to abide in us and so do devils, but they cannot abide in places that are filled with the Spirit of God. Whenever Jesus came into natural temples the demons fled. When we allow the light of Jesus Christ to abide in us, darkness must flee! This is why God tells us in the Book of Revelation that He would rather for us to be hot or cold. He says that he will spit anything that is lukewarm out of His mouth.

Devils…cannot abide in places that are filled with the Spirit of God.

Lukewarm means "mixture." When we mix hot and cold (in the natural) we get *warm*. When we try to mix Jesus and the devil (in the spirit) we get *lukewarm*. The Greek interpretation of the word *hot* means to be fervent for the Lord. The word *cold* is *psuchros* in the Greek. It is closely related to the Greek word *psuche*, and it is defined as "the rational mind." *Psuche* is related to the English word *psyche*. To be cold means to be totally carnally minded. God wants us to be totally sold out to Him or totally carnally minded, but not in-between.

5. **Lay eggs.** I mentioned the cockatrice spirit in an earlier chapter. Isaiah 59:5–7 says:

"They hatch cockatrice eggs, and weave the spider's web: he that eateth of their eggs dieth, and that which is crushed breaketh out into a viper. Their webs shall not become garment, neither shall they cover themselves with their works: their works are works of iniquity, and the act of violence is in their hands. Their feet run to do evil, and they make haste to shed innocent blood: their thoughts are thoughts of iniquity; wasting and destruction are in their paths."

Once when I was at a prayer watch at midnight, the Lord spoke to me that I was to make the rebels walk the plank. This word caught me so off guard; I thought all was well. God said I was to put the sword of the word to their backs and make them walk the plank. I had no idea what the Holy Spirit was speaking about at the time. I shared the word with a couple of intercessors and moved on.

As I began to question the intercessors about our midnight assignment, I noticed a breach in the wall. God had given me specific instructions to call the entire congregation on a consecration. Everyone was given special prayer instructions. As I questioned everyone about their prayer assignments, a young woman told me God had instructed her to do something else. When I tried to correct her on the issue, she became even more resistant. I told her that this was not her private time with the Lord to pray as she desired, but she was on a specific intercessory assignment on the behalf of the church.

She continued to tell me that God told her to do something else. This is a perfect example of rebellion. It is as the sin of witchcraft. Rebellion against constituted authority is spiritually mutiny. This young woman was a very gifted vessel. The more gifted we are in God, the greater need we have for true submission. False submission is a spirit that causes people to go out of their way to paint a picture of submission at any cost. This spirit usually causes people to overdo their assignments or obligations. They always need to spotlight every act of service because ultimately they need praise for what they have done. Their goal is to hide their true state of rebellion behind the guise of false submission.

Rebellion against constituted authority is spiritually mutiny.

I did not deal with this young woman as sternly as I should have. The repercussions were that she was a part of eight families leaving our church. Though this person eventually returned and is still with us today, the eggs she laid caused many to fall by the way side. The good news is that every person who left always stirred up confusion and kept me distracted with their problems. When they left, the problems followed them out the door.

But we began to get threatening letters, and public slanderous statements were made on our website. God would show me the faces of the people who committed these acts as I read the notes. They looked like robots being controlled, and their eyes were deeply evil. The manifestation of the cockatrice spirit was evident in their lives. As we have read Isaiah 59:5–7, let us review the manifestations.

- ↬ They spin webs of confusion (v. 5).

- ↬ Their works are works of iniquity (v. 6).

- ↬ They cause spiritual death to the people who eat of their eggs (v. 5).

- ↬ Acts of violence are in their hands (v. 6).

- ↬ Their feet are quick to run to evil (v. 7).

- ↬ They do not hesitate to shed innocent blood (v. 7).

- ↬ Their thoughts are of iniquity (v. 7).

- ↬ Waste and destruction are in their path (v. 7).

The offspring of the rebellious are doubly hellish.

The ruling spirit of the cockatrice strongman manifests in the eyes. Most times when we pray for people in deliverance sessions, the spirit manifests itself through the character of the demon. For example, Leviathan's strength is in the neck, and we have seen physical manifestations of necks enlarging in size as the spirit left the person's body. The cockatrice manifests itself in the eyes of a person. I have seen young women's eyes swell two to three inches from their faces as a result of the spirit leaving their body. The cockatrice spirit is dangerous to the body of Christ, but the eggs they produce are even more dangerous. The offspring of the rebellious are doubly hellish. Jesus made this comment to the religiously rebellious folk of His day.

The revelation of the snake season did not come to me easily. I thought I was preaching about something that was happening to somebody else. I could not understand the depths of this kind of attack until it happened to me personally. I have a very good friend in ministry who experienced a Judas manifestation in his camp. He was literally torn to pieces and put back together again. Though I listened to his story, my mind could not imagine his pain. God took all questions out of my mind concerning this issue. No one could ever tell me what I was about to learn for myself.

As I preached the message "Snake Season" in my own church, it seemed as if I tapped into another realm. God clearly showed me that He was about to remove anyone from around me who was not right. He called it a spiritual showdown! God had moved so many people already. My flesh was not ready for another move of God like this, but my spirit submitted to His words. I began to feel uneasy about a particular leader in our church. I trusted him so much that it baffled my natural mind; I did not understand why I felt this way.

I approached him several times with my concern, but he assured me that everything was all right. As my subliminal suspicions began to manifest themselves before my very eyes, I realized that the number one person I depended on in ministry began to lie to me. I was not the only one who noticed. Several ministers came to me with concerns about this minister and the way he was carrying himself. I was so embarrassed that I

could not immediately go to him and tell him that we
had caught him in several blatant lies. I had to give
myself time to catch up with what was going on. Four of
my primary leaders privately came to me with the same
story. My right-hand man was trying to turn them
against me and the ministry.

Truly it was snake season, but I was not ready for
the venom the enemy had loosed. Confirmation after
confirmation came my way. By this time, this person I
trusted avoided all conversations with me. God was
blessing in so many ways. I was leaving messages of
praise reports on his phone with no response coming
back to me. The last time I talked with him to share
good and bad news, he hurried me off the phone to say
he would call back. The last time I heard his voice it
seemed cold and unconcerned about what I was saying.

I knew this was a manifestation of the cold-blooded
cockatrice. This spirit could turn fifty years of friend-
ship into a nightmare. I finally shared with him that I
knew the devil was trying to make him leave the church.
I literally begged him to let me pray for him before the
congregation and let them know he was leaving. I asked
him, "Please do not leave with anything negative in your
heart!" He would not admit that he was leaving. A local
prophet came to the Sunday morning service immediately after we had this conversation.

My close brother in the Lord was under so much
attack from the enemy, when I gave an altar call for
people to "get their lives right with God" he came to the
altar. I did not know how to respond. This was not an
altar call for healing or a financial blessing. It was a
serious call for those who were not right with God.

Because I did not know how to respond, the local prophet picked up the baton. He stood in front of the broken minister and prophesied that the devil was trying to put him out of place. This was an answer to my prayer! Surely this was the confirmation that my leader needed to know this was not the time for him to leave. I rejoiced in my soul!

After service we went downstairs and ministered deliverance to a woman. The woman was miraculously set free. When I looked into the eyes of the leader that I knew the devil wanted to move, I knew that everything was going to be all right. The next day he called me and shared something with me that I will never forget.

He told me that the same prophet who prophesied to him had an open vision: There were twelve demons sitting around a conference table laughing uncontrollably. They insisted that their plan would work. They said they would not bother Kim and Ardell anymore. They would get my main leader and the leader under him. These spirits had on black coats, and they had black velvet hoods in their hands. Inside the hoods were "cloudiness," "blurriness," "division" and "conspiracy." The demons were dispatched against Spoken Word Ministries, with the head demon assigned against my main leader. The assignment was that the devil would use the closest person to me to take the other leaders out, and I would never know it until it was too late! This was supposed to tear me apart and discourage me in the ministry.

I thank God for the prophetic word of the Lord! It saved our church. If it had not been for the prophetic warning, we would have overlooked the plan of the enemy. When he came, we saw him clearly. Truly I could sing the song, "Devil, boo...I see you"! As the minister under attack approached the others with words of divisiveness, they all came to me to share their concern. We later found out that our leader, who we all loved and respected, packed his things in the middle of the night and left. He pretended to take a short leave to get off with the Lord, but had been planning for months to leave the ministry.

When none of our calls were returned for weeks, we finally accepted the fact that one of our key leaders had walked off from the ministry. My husband and I were baffled because we never got the opportunity to sit down and talk to him. The hardest thing for me to accept was that he did not take heed to the word of the Lord spoken through the prophet. This minister had a huge financial opportunity, and he had to make a choice between the ministry and his opportunity. He chose the opportunity. During the time that we were trying to call this minister and he would not return our calls, I had a dream.

I dreamed that he came back from "his opportunity" and was running around the church like nothing had happened. I asked him how things went with his venture. He frowned and responded that things did not turn out as he expected. He walked into the bathroom, fell on his belly like a snake and crawled unto the door of the stall. As his body stood erect in the stall, urine came down his legs.

While I was away on the road, my dream manifested before the eyes of my leaders. I told them of the dream, and just as I dreamed it, the minister in question really showed up at the church. He was running around doing the things he always had done during the service. He grabbed the offering from the finance team as he had always done. As he looked into the eyes of the other leaders, tears welled up in his eyes as he asked, "Have I done anything wrong?" (I hate the devil.) He threw the offering on the table and walked out of the church. He did not have to pack because he had already packed in the middle of the night when no one was around.

He has not returned since that time. He left all of the ministry work in shambles. The work that only he did was left for us to put back together like a jigsaw puzzle. Without even a note, we had to figure out the work he alone was responsible for. No one else knew what he did. The difficult part was that we did not even get a one-day notice. I must admit that it hurt when I heard that people were taking up offerings for him when they heard "what happened to him." It was made to look as though we cast him out of the church with nothing after he had faithfully served so many years.

The race only goes to those who endure to the end.

The Word of the Lord tells us that the race only goes to those who endure to the end. People who did great works for the Lord lost their souls and ended up in hell. I believe God will restore this mighty man of God and use him greatly. Although the devil used him, he was only a victim and a casualty of war. By the way, "the opportunity" that I believe was the main tool of the enemy to pull him out of the church did not manifest in the time that it was supposed to. What does it profit a man to gain the whole world and lose his soul?

Please do not judge this person; only pray for him! The Bible tells us that if it were possible, the very elect will be deceived. Some of my acquaintances who are new in deliverance ministry simply did not understand. They asked, "How can the devil get the demon-busters like this?" My only response to this question was that Jesus was the greatest demon-buster who ever existed; if Judas betrayed Him, why should we think we cannot be betrayed?

Illegitimate enemies are just a waste of time.

I thank God that just as Jesus knew Judas was about to leave, God revealed the plans of the devil through this leader to me. I have come to understand that it is all right to have enemies close to you as long as they are legitimate. I would often wonder how I could have so many enemies sit so close up under me. God revealed to me recently that it was all right as long as they were "legitimate enemies," which are enemies sent by God. I do not have time for illegitimate enemies. When I pass the test of having a legitimate enemy in my camp, I get a reward. Illegitimate enemies are just a waste of time. They are frivolous, petty and nitpicking, and we get nothing for putting up with people God has not called us to endure.

If I am going to have an enemy close to me, I may as well have a legal one sent by God. When this is the case, we can respond to Judas (a type of "apostolic enemy) as Jesus did and tell him to do what he was sent to do.

The enemy desires to sift our leaders like wheat.

We should never be afraid to minister deliverance to our leaders. Jesus had to rebuke the devil out of Peter. The enemy desires to sift our leaders like wheat. A week before I knew what was going on I had a vision in my sleep of a giant silver sifter that was full of human beings. There were two levels under their feet. The first level represented their relationship with God. Under that was another level, which was the church. God moved the bottom level (the church), and the people began to fall through.

I sat up out of my sleep and yelled with a loud voice, "It is a sifting!" I startled my husband, and he was awakened. It was so real! God showed me that people who have a foundation in the church and have no foundational relationship with God personally will fall through the cracks. I believe a maturity took place in Peter's life after he was separated from Jesus physically.

Peter's walk with Jesus in the earthly realm represents a type of connection with the church. During this time Peter was not strong enough to resist the temptations of the enemy. It is almost like a mother eagle throwing her baby out of the nest to learn how to fly. We so easily quote the scripture in Isaiah, "Mounting up with wings as eagles," but do we consider what it is like to fly for the first time? When Jesus left, Peter had to grow up! It is not difficult to detect immaturity when the enemy puts the pressure on high.

Jesus had imparted all He had into Peter; now he had to walk in what he had received. If Jesus would have remained with Peter, he would have never won all the souls recorded in the Book of Acts; he would have been waiting on Jesus to do it. This is the state of most believers today. They are waiting on Jesus to do it!

Jesus said He has given us the keys to do the greater works. Often the church can become a type of spiritual crutch to believers. The enemy has tricked us into becoming spiritually stuffed. We come into spiritual filling stations every Sunday and one weekday, and we get our tanks filled. The sad part is that we never drive anywhere to use the gas we have received.

The enemy has tricked us into becoming spiritually stuffed.

Many Christians are nailed to the seats of the church. They only know the pastoral spirit of Jesus, the one that immediately watches over our every step and feeds us until we are full. People cannot relate to the apostolic spirit of Christ that sends and releases us to do what has been already imparted into us. The end-time believers must have a release, or we will blow up. This can be done only through the apostolic valve of God. This release will cause the sent ones to walk in another level of spiritual maturity.

We cannot make it without the church, but even that must be placed in its right perspective. Those who have no true relationship with Christ will be the believer's bait for the enemy. Jesus told Peter, "Before the cock crows three times, you will deny that you ever knew Me." (See Matthew 26:34.) If we think we are so spiritual that the devil can never deceive us, we only deceive ourselves. We must be careful that when we think we stand, we do not fall.

Those who have no true relationship with Christ will be the believer's bait for the enemy.

By the way, it would not be fair to share my trauma without sharing my testimony. For every person who walked out the door, two more walked in. When my closest leader left the ministry, we only had four people on our staff. Within a month's time, our staff grew to fifteen faithful people. Everything shifted into the will of the Lord. Like a matrix game, one person was moved, and everyone else fell in place. It was a "blessing in disguise." What looked like a curse, after walking it out, became my blessing! I pray that you will be encouraged by my story and allow God to take you "from a mess to a miracle" too.

CONCLUSION

In closing, I would like to say to all the new believers, old-timers and short-timers (those about to backslide): Jesus is coming back soon! This is the time to gird up and go forward. "Go forward," says the Lord! All old things have passed away, and all things have become new. As you press toward the mark of the high calling there will be much persecution. If you are not experiencing much persecution for the name of Jesus, turn around and run—you are going in the wrong direction!

I pray that the testimonies in this book have inspired you to go on and that the teachings have challenged you to come up higher. My word of encouragement to you is that you *can* have your cake and eat it too! Let me ask you this question: Why would you want a cake you cannot eat? Why would you want a promise you can never experience? This is why we must learn the importance of posterity over prosperity. Prosperity is good, but when we set our goals on posterity, the promises that we never live to see will be realized by our seed! Glory to God.

If you are not experiencing much persecution for the name of Jesus, turn around and run—you are going in the wrong direction!

Cake that is never eaten represents stale faith. Stale faith is still faith, or faith that gets tired of waiting on God. Anything that sits still is lying dormant. Nevertheless, dormant waters run deep. The Bible tells us that rivers of living water will flow out of our bellies. Whatever you do in life, never be comfortable where you are. God always has a next level for you, a place called next! When something is stale it becomes impaired in vigor and ineffective. The results are barren grounds that lack reproductive ability. God commands us to be fruitful.

Stale faith is... faith that gets tired of waiting on God.

Conclusion

We have a responsibility to believe God until the end. No matter what the circumstances look like, there are more for us than there ever can be against us. The four lepers in 2 Kings 7 did not have still faith. They got up out of their problem and went toward the answer. The captain at the gate of Samaria questioned God. He asked, "Could God do this thing?" The prophet had already spoken on the behalf of the Lord. He told the evil captain, "You will see God do it, but you will not taste of it." In other words, he said the captain could not have his cake and eat it too.

People are compromising because they cannot wait on God long enough to believe Him.

The spirit of compromise has been loosed in the land. People are compromising because they cannot wait on God long enough to believe Him. Some who started out with us are not around to experience what God promised. It was not just my promise, but a promise for those who were around us. The prophet spoke over the entire city of Samaria, yet the lepers heard the word and received it for themselves. Receive this word for yourself: About this time tomorrow the blessing of the Lord will be running the people of God down and taking them over in the body of Christ.

Stand still and see the salvation of the Lord. Do not be blown away by every wind of doctrine or move out of place by spirits of error and offense. This is your season, but you must know it for yourself. Yes, the enemy may come in, but it is the will of God to use tribulation to raise the standard in your life. You are in the best place you could ever be—the body of Christ. Though we may have trouble on every side, there is no place like home (the church). You just need strength to endure so God can bring you from your mess to your miracle.

Remember, if you believe and never compromise, you can have your cake and eat it too!

From the Heart of

Apostle Kim Daniels

TO GOD BE THE GLORY FOR THE GREAT
THINGS HE HAS DONE

To Contact the Author:

Mail: Kimberly Daniels
            P.O. Box 40278
            Jacksonville, FL 32203-0278

Phone: (904) 908-4261 or (904) 791-4345

Fax: (904) 598-1412

Email: apostlekd@bustadevil.com

Website: KimberlyDaniels.com